...be ...d on or ... the

For a complete listing of all our titles in this area please visit **he.palgrave.com/study-skills**

Cite Them Right

The Essential Referencing Guide

Tenth revised and expanded edition

Richard Pears & Graham Shields

Previous editions published 2004, 2005 and 2008 by Pear Tree Books

Eighth edition 2010
Ninth edition 2013
Tenth edition 2016

Published by
PALGRAVE

Palgrave in the UK is an imprint of Macmillan Publishers Limited, registered in England, company number 785998, of 4 Crinan Street, London, N1 9XW.

Palgrave is a global imprint of the above company and is represented throughout the world.

Palgrave® and Macmillan® are registered trademarks in the United States, the United Kingdom, Europe and other countries.

ISBN: 978-1-137-58504-2   paperback

This book is printed on paper suitable for recycling and made from fully managed and sustained forest sources. Logging, pulping and manufacturing processes are expected to conform to the environmental regulations of the country of origin.

A catalogue record for this book is available from the British Library.

Contents

Section F APA referencing style 91

Section G   Chicago referencing style

Section H MHRA referencing style **121**

Section I **MLA referencing style** **131**

Foreword

Welcome to the revised and expanded tenth edition of *Cite them right*. We have reached a milestone in that it has now been in existence for 25 years. It began life as little more than a single sheet of A4 paper offering guidance on how to reference basic printed sources such as textbooks and journal articles. Nowadays, the vast range of information available and the rapid developments in electronic publishing and devices mean that continual updating is required. This edition bears witness to that need.

Our book strives to be comprehensive and cover all possible sources for referencing in every academic discipline. Our experience in university libraries with students and academics has allowed us to understand more clearly where students struggle with referencing. In many instances, their queries fuel the need to clarify or refine examples and, in some cases, create new ones. We are therefore grateful to our readers for their continuing feedback and reviews on the usefulness of *Cite them right*. Your many positive reviews encourage us. We hope that you will continue to provide constructive suggestions in the future.

New and revised material

A number of major revisions and expanded sections have been added, including a new legal sources section in Harvard style and a new chapter for the Chicago referencing style. Other revisions include:

- Fully expanded APA/MHRA/MLA/OSCOLA/Vancouver sections
- Serials section
- What is referencing?
- Computer/video games
- Secondary referencing

- Citing and referencing multiple authors
- Later and revised editions
- Referencing journal articles in virtual learning environments.

Many new sources have been added to this edition, namely:
- Mobile apps
- Mood boards
- MOOCs
- Clip art
- *Instagram*
- *FaceTime*
- Annuals
- Facsimile editions
- Use of hashtags # in social media
- Chinese/Arabic fonts
- Citing long corporate names
- Quoting from non-English material
- The use of anecdotal and personal information
- Conference papers and whole proceedings in journals.

How to make the best use of *Cite them right*

You should not be daunted by the number of pages in this book – you are *not* expected to read it from cover to cover.

Everyone should read **Sections A–D** which cover the basics about referencing, quotations and avoiding plagiarism. These will provide you with a much clearer understanding of where you can find the elements that need to be referenced, and the confidence to set them out correctly in your text and reference list.

Section E, the main body of the book, details a comprehensive range of source materials and provides specific examples of how they should be referenced using the Harvard (author-date) referencing style. This system originated in the USA but has become the most widely used referencing style internationally, due to its simplicity and ease of use. However, there is no single authority to define 'Harvard'; hence there are many versions, with slight variations, of the system in use. The alternative title, 'author-date', arises from the fact that the in-text citations follow the format of using the author's surname and the date of publication (where available) to link with the full reference details in the reference list/bibliography.

Use the **Contents** or **Index** pages to identify the type of source you need to reference (for example ebook, web page, government publication), then follow the advice and example(s) on the relevant page(s).

Sections F–K provide examples for referencing the most commonly used sources in the American Psychological Association (APA), Chicago, Modern Humanities Research Association (MHRA), Modern Language Association (MLA), Oxford University Standard for Citation of Legal Authorities (OSCOLA) and Vancouver styles.

A **Glossary** is included to explain the meaning of certain terms used in the text. These words appear in bold when they first occur within each section.

Richard Pears and Graham Shields, 2016

Acknowledgements

The authors would like to thank:

The House of Commons Information Office for permission to quote from *Factsheet G17. The Official Report*. Information on the updated citation of *Written questions and answers* kindly provided by Debbie Cesvette.

Colleagues at Durham University and the University of Cumbria for their advice, and in particular Mamtimyn Sunuodula, Area Studies librarian, Durham University Library.

Scott Winstanley for his advice relating to video games.

Staff and students at other academic institutions for their support, constructive feedback and suggestions.

Section A
What is referencing?

Referencing is the process of acknowledging other people's work when you have used it in your assignment or research. It allows the reader to locate your source material as quickly and easily as possible so that they can read these sources themselves and verify the validity of your arguments. Referencing provides the link between what you write and the evidence on which it is based.

You identify the sources that you have used by citing them in the text of your assignment (called **citations** or **in-text citations**) and referencing them at the end of your assignment (called the **reference list** or **end-text citations**). The reference list only includes the sources cited in your text. It is not the same thing as a **bibliography**, which uses the same referencing style, but also includes all material, for example background readings, used in the preparation of your work.

Why reference?

There are a number of important reasons why you need to reference. Referencing allows you to:

- Demonstrate that you have read widely on the subject and considered and evaluated the writings of others
- Show your tutor the evidence of your research and thereby appreciate your contribution to the topic
- Establish the credibility and authority of your ideas and arguments
- Enable the reader to locate the original material you used
- Give credit to the original author/creator

- Enable the reader to form their own views on the value of your sources and how you have interpreted them
- Distinguish between your own ideas and opinions and those of others
- Highlight relevant points by quoting, paraphrasing or summarising from the original text (see Section C)
- Achieve a better mark or grade
- Avoid **plagiarism** (see below).

Every academic institution requires its students to reference in their work and your tutors will expect you to do this accurately, clearly and concisely. Your university or institution should issue you with guidelines on how they expect you to reference in your particular subject area. Follow these guidelines carefully.

When should you reference?

You are expected to reference every time you use someone else's work or ideas in your own work. There are no exceptions to this rule and it applies to all your work, including assignments, essays, presentations, dissertations and other research or publications. It is very important that when undertaking your research you systematically record and save full details of all the resources that you have used, and it is vital that you save these sources at the time that you use them. Otherwise, it can be very difficult (or even impossible) to locate these resources again at a later date.

What should you reference?

You should reference **all the sources** that you use for your assignment or research and maintain records for all of them. Any information that you copy and paste, repeat word-for-word, paraphrase or summarise must be acknowledged by referencing it. This includes all information available on the

internet. Students commonly believe, erroneously, that because it is available online they are not required to acknowledge it. There are numerous reference management software tools available (some free) that can help you to manage the referencing process. Be aware though, that even if you use these tools you must still double-check your citations and references to ensure that they appear in a consistent style and follow your institution's/tutor's guidelines.

Your aim should always be to reference reliable sources of information. These may include books (printed and ebooks), journal articles, web pages, conference papers, newspaper articles, lecture notes, government publications, videos, legal material and reports. This list can be extended, depending on the subject you are studying and the nature of the source material in your area.

You need to consider how reliable the sources are, because newspaper and magazine articles, websites, wikis and popular or social media can be unreliable or weak sources of information. They may simply offer someone's opinion on a topic. Always try to locate academic sources that substantiate the original material. In many cases this may be peer-reviewed books or articles (also referred to as 'refereed' or 'scholarly'). This means that they are written by experts in their field and then reviewed by several other experts (or editorial board) to ensure quality and accuracy before the material is published.

Students often struggle to understand which version of a source they should reference. You should always reference the version of the information source that you have actually used (see also Secondary referencing section below). The reason for this is clear – a journal or newspaper article may appear in both print and electronic formats and the two versions may vary.

If you have included an appendix in your assignment or research it should be clearly labelled with a letter (A) or number (1). If it contains information from other sources, these should be cited in-text in the appendix with full references given at the end of the appendix as a separate reference list.

What about secondary referencing?

In some cases you may want to refer to a source that is mentioned or quoted in the work you are reading. This is known as **secondary referencing**. It is important that, whenever possible, you cite and reference the primary source of your information. For example, if you read about a study by Harvey (primary source) in a book by Lewis (secondary source) you should try to locate and read the original work by Harvey. This will enable you to check for yourself that Harvey has not been misinterpreted or misquoted by Lewis. If you cannot locate the primary source (in this case Harvey), you cannot include it in your reference list. You can only cite it in your text. In your essay or assignment, you should cite both sources and use the phrase 'quoted in' or 'cited in', depending on whether the author of the secondary source is directly quoting or summarising from the primary source.

Examples

Harvey (2015, quoted in Lewis, 2016, p. 86) provides an excellent survey …

White's views on genetic abnormalities in crops (2014, cited in Murray, 2015) support the idea that …

You then include Lewis and Murray in your reference list (and Harvey and White if you have read them).

Once again, if you are unable to read the primary sources you can only cite them (as in the examples).

What about referencing common knowledge?

There is no need to reference things which are considered **common knowledge**. This is generally defined as facts, dates, events and information that are expected to be known by someone studying or working in a particular subject area or field. The information or facts can be found in numerous places and are likely to be widely known: for example, that London is the capital city of England. Such information does not generally have to be referenced.

However, as a student, you may have only just started to study a particular subject and be unaware of what is regarded as common knowledge. In order to decide if the material you want to include in your work constitutes common knowledge, you need to ask yourself the following questions:

- Did I know this information before I started my course?
- Did this information or idea come from my own brain?

If the answer to either or both of these questions is 'no', then the information is not common knowledge to you. In these cases you should cite and reference the sources. So, if you are unsure whether something is common knowledge, it is always advisable to cite and reference it.

What about referencing anecdotal or personal experience?

Anecdotal sources can be very compelling, particularly in the field of medicine. The primary weakness of anecdotes and personal stories is that they cannot be verified. Although, in most cases, you would not reference anecdotal sources of information, you may still use these sources, and include them as an appendix to your main text. It is very important that you are aware of confidentiality and are absolutely certain that you have permission to use the material (see more about confidential information below). Clearly, if you have recorded someone recounting their story or anecdote then you can include the transcript as an appendix to your work (with the interviewee's permission).

You can speak from personal experience in contexts like personal responses, opinion pieces or reflective papers, and in many subjects this approach is positively encouraged and expected. Experience and opinions are important in your writing because a large part of academic writing is demonstrating that you have understood the foundation of knowledge on which your contributions stand. Once again though, to back up your opinions or responses you should always try to support your viewpoints and experiences with substantiating scholarly material.

What about referencing confidential information?

There may be times when you need to use a source of information that is confidential, for example medical, legal or business material. This information is, by its very nature, unpublished and not in the public domain. In most cases, your tutor will offer guidance on whether you can use the information and reference it. If you decide to use confidential sources you should always obtain permission from those who might be affected by its inclusion in your work. Similarly, it is regarded as good practice to ask for permission from the sender of information via personal communications (see Section E24).

In some cases, you may be able to anonymise the documents or sources, allowing you to refer to them for argument or statistical purposes. For example, in healthcare subjects you could use terms like 'Patient X' or 'Placement hospital'. See Section E4.5 for more details on how to reference confidential information.

What is plagiarism?

Plagiarism is a term that can often frighten students. It conjures up all kinds of negative thoughts and yet it is relatively easy to avoid by following good academic practice. The term itself describes the unacknowledged use of someone else's work. This includes material or ideas from any (published or unpublished) sources, whether print, electronic (even if freely available on the internet) or audiovisual. Using the words or ideas of others without citing and referencing them would be construed as plagiarism and is a very serious academic offence. At the end of the day, it is regarded as the stealing of intellectual property.

The following are all considered forms of plagiarism:

- Presenting any part of someone else's work (including the work of other students) as your own
- Using a source of information word-for-word (without quotation marks)
- Paraphrasing or summarising material in your assignment without acknowledging the original source through in-text citation and reference (see Section C)

- 'Recycling' a piece of your own work that you have previously submitted for another module or course (that is, self-plagiarism)
- Citing and referencing sources that you have not used.

How can you avoid plagiarism?

Universities use a series of sophisticated software applications and other methods to detect incidences of plagiarism in students' work. In most cases, students plagiarise unintentionally. Poor organisation and time management, as well as a failure to understand good academic practice or follow the published university guidelines, are often to blame. Through rigorous preparation and careful checking of your institution's advice and guidelines on referencing, you should be confident that you will not be accused of plagiarising.

The following advice can help:

- Manage your time and plan your work – ensure that you give yourself enough time to prepare, read and write
- Maintain clear notes and records of all the sources you use as you use them – it can prove very difficult to locate sources later
- Be organised – keep all of your notes and references until your assignment has been graded/marked
- When paraphrasing an author's text, ensure that you use your own words and a sentence structure that is sufficiently different from the original text (see Section C)
- In your notes, highlight in colour/bold any **direct quotations** you want to use in your assignment – this will help to ensure that you use quotation marks alongside an appropriate reference when you are writing up your work

- Allow enough time to check your final draft for possible referencing errors or omissions: for example, check that all your in-text citations have a corresponding entry in your reference list, and vice versa.

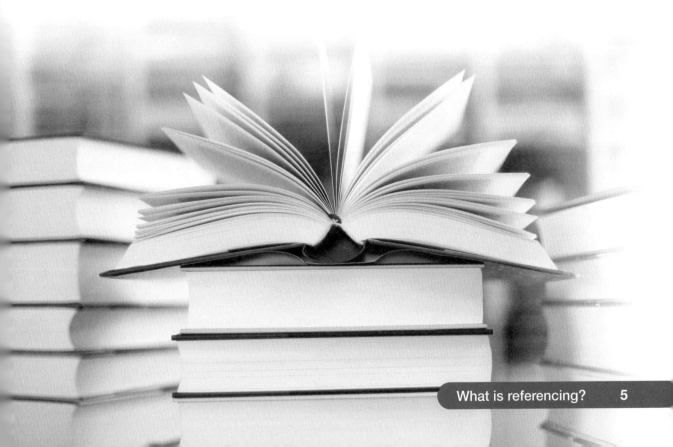

Section B
How to cite

Setting out citations

When you cite you are referring to someone else's work or ideas in the text of your essay or assignment. It is often called **in-text citing**.

It is important to remember that **citations** in your assignments must be included in the final word count.

In-text citations give the brief (abbreviated) details of the work that you are quoting from, or to which you are referring in your text. These citations will then link to the full **reference** in the **reference list** at the end of your work, which is arranged in alphabetical order by author. Works cited in appendices, but not in the main body of your text, should be included in a separate reference list at the end of your appendix. It is important to note that **footnotes** and **endnotes** are not used in Harvard and other author-date referencing styles.

There are several ways in which you can incorporate citations into your text, depending on your own style and the flow of the work. However, a tutor or supervisor may advise you on their preferred format. You can see from the examples below how you can vary the use of citations in your text.

Your citations should include the following elements:

* Author(s) or editor(s) surname/family name
* Year of publication
* Page number(s) if required (always required for **direct quotations**).

If you are quoting directly or using ideas from a specific page or pages of a work, you should include the page number(s) in your citations. Insert the abbreviation p. (or pp.) before the page number(s).

> **Example**
>
> Harris (2014, p. 56) argued that 'nursing staff ...'

If your citation refers to a complete work or to ideas that run through an entire work, your citation would simply use the author and date details.

> **Example**
>
> In a recent study (Evans, 2015), qualifications of school-leavers were analysed ...

Citing one author/editor

Cite the author/editor.

> **Example**
>
> In his autobiography (Fry, 2014) ...

Citing a corporate author

Cite the name (or initials, if well known) of the corporate body. For corporate bodies with long names where you wish to make clear what its initials stand for, you should write out the name in full the first time you use it and use the abbreviation for the citation. Be consistent in using the abbreviation each time to ensure that all your references appear correctly in your reference list.

> **Examples**
>
> ... as shown in its annual report (BBC, 2016).
>
> ... the popularity of visiting historical monuments (English Heritage, 2014).
>
> ... in claims made by the United Nations Framework Conference of Climate Change (UNFCCC, 2014) ...

Citing two authors/editors

Both are listed.

> **Example**
>
> Recent educational research (Lewis and Jones, 2012) …

Citing three authors/editors

All three are listed.

> **Example**
>
> In an important study of the subject (Hill, Smith and Reid, 2014) …

Citing four or more authors/editors

Cite the first name listed in the source followed by *et al*. (meaning 'and others').

> **Example**
>
> `In-text citation`
>
> New research on health awareness by Tipton *et al*. (2016) …

NB You would either do exactly the same in your reference list, for example:

Tipton, C. *et al*. (2016) …

OR, if your **institution requires referencing of all named authors**:

Tipton, C., Howell, P., Richards, S., Ince, V., and Emery, L. (2016) …

If you are writing for a publication, you should follow the editor's guidelines, as you may be required to name all the authors, regardless of the number, to ensure that each author's contribution is recognised.

Citing a source with no author/editor

Where the name of an author/editor cannot be found, use the title (in italics). Do not use 'Anon.' or 'Anonymous'.

> **Example**
>
> In a groundbreaking survey (*Health of the nation*, 2011) …

Citing multiple sources

If you need to refer to two or more publications at the same time, these can be separated by semicolons (;). The publications should be cited in chronological order (with the earliest date first). If more than one work is published in the same year, then they should be listed alphabetically by author/editor.

> **Example**
>
> A number of environmental studies (Town, 2009; Williams, 2009; Andrews *et al.*, 2011; Martin and Richards, 2013) considered …

Citing sources published in the same year by the same author

Sometimes you may need to cite two (or more) publications by an author published in the same year. To distinguish between the items in the text, allocate lower-case letters in alphabetical order after the publication date.

> **Example**
>
> In his study of the work of Rubens, Miller (2006a) emphasised the painter's mastery of drama. However, his final analysis on this subject (Miller, 2006b) argued that …

In your reference list, the publications would look like this.

> **Example**
>
> Miller, S. (2006a) *The Flemish masters*. London: Phaidon Press.
>
> Miller, S. (2006b) *Rubens and his art*. London: Killington Press.

Citing different editions of the same work by the same author

Separate the dates of publication with a semicolon (;) with the earliest date first.

> **Example**
>
> In both editions (Hawksworth, 2009; 2013) …

Citing sources with multiple authors

If you want to cite a book edited by Holmes and Baker, which has, for example, ten contributors and does not specify who wrote each section or chapter, follow the format of citing using the editors' names.

> **Example**
>
> Recent research (Holmes and Baker, 2009, pp. 411–428) proved …

NB See Section E1.9 (Chapters/sections of edited books) for the relevant information on citing and referencing when the author's name is given for a specific chapter or section.

Citing a source with no date

Use the phrase 'no date'.

> **Example**
>
> In an interesting survey of youth participation in sport, the authors (Harvey and Williams, no date) …

Citing a source with no author or date

Use the title and 'no date'.

> **Example**
>
> Integrated transport systems clearly work (*Trends in European transport systems*, no date).

Citing a web page

If you are citing a **web page**, it should follow the preceding guidelines, citing by author and date where possible; by title and date if there is no identifiable author; or, as in the example, by **URL** if neither author nor title can be identified.

> **Example**
>
> The latest survey of health professionals (http://www.onlinehealthsurvey.org, 2015) reveals that …

For more details on how to cite and reference web pages, see Section E8 (The internet).

Section C
How to quote, paraphrase and summarise

Setting out quotations

Quotations should be relevant to your arguments and used judiciously in your text. Excessive use of quotations can disrupt the flow of your writing and prevent you from demonstrating your understanding and analysis of the sources you have read. Your tutor will prefer to read your own interpretation of the evidence.

Bear in mind that **direct quotations** are also counted in your assignment's total word count.

Short direct quotations (up to two or three lines) should be enclosed in quotation marks (single or double – be consistent) and included in the body of your text. Give the author, date and page number(s)/URL that the quotation was taken from.

Example

'If you need to illustrate the idea of nineteenth-century America as a land of opportunity, you could hardly improve on the life of Albert Michelson' (Bryson, 2004, p. 156).

Longer quotations should be entered as a separate paragraph and indented from the main text. Quotation marks are not required.

Example

King describes the intertwining of fate and memory in many evocative passages, such as:

So the three of them rode towards their end of the Great Road, while summer lay all about them, breathless as a gasp. Roland looked up and saw something that made him forget all about the Wizard's Rainbow. It was his mother, leaning out of her apartment's bedroom window: the oval of her face surrounded by the timeless gray stone of the castle's west wing (King, 1997, pp. 553–554).

Quoting material not in English

You should always quote in the language which appears in the source that you are reading. Cite the original author and use quotation marks (or indent for longer quotes as above).

Example

'… que nunca sabemos lo que tenemos hasta que se nos ha escapado' (Delibes, 2010).

If quoting from a translated work you should cite the original author and quote the text in the language in which it appears in the item you are reading.

Example

In-text citation

'Daniel realised that his future was inextricably linked with his village' (Delibes, 2013).

Reference list

Delibes, M. (2013) *The path*. Translated by J. and B. Haycraft. London: Dolphin Books.

If you translate some foreign language text into English yourself and include it in your work, you should not present this as a quotation. However, you must acknowledge the original source.

> **Example**
>
> **In-text citation**
>
> Delibes notes that you do not know what you have until it is gone (Delibes, 2010, p. 56).
>
> **Reference list**
>
> Delibes, M. (2010) *El camino*. Madrid: Destino.

Making changes to quotations

Omitting part of a quotation

Indicate this by using three dots … (called an **ellipsis**).

> **Example**
>
> 'Drug prevention … efforts backed this up' (Gardner, 2007, p. 49).

Inserting your own, or different, words into a quotation

Put them in square brackets [ ].

> **Example**
>
> 'In this field [crime prevention], community support officers …' (Higgins, 2008, p. 17).

Pointing out an error in a quotation

Do not correct the error; instead write [*sic*].

> **Example**
>
> Williams (2008, p. 86) noted that 'builders maid [*sic*] bricks'.

Retaining/modernising historical spellings

Decide to either retain the original spelling or modernise the spelling, and note this in your text.

> **Examples**
>
> 'Hast thou not removed one Grain of Dirt or Rhubbish?' (Kent, 1727, p. 2).
>
> 'Have you not removed one grain of dirt or rubbish?' (Kent, 1727, p. 2, spelling modernised).

Emphasising part of a quotation

Put the words you want to emphasise in italics and state that you have added the emphasis.

> **Example**
>
> 'Large numbers of *women* are more prepared to support eco-friendly projects' (Denby, 2014, p. 78, my emphasis).

If the original text uses italics, state that the italics are in the original source.

> **Example**
>
> 'The dictionary is based on *rigorous analysis* of the grammar of the language' (Soanes, 2015, p. 2, original emphasis).

Paraphrasing

When you **paraphrase**, you express someone else's writing in your own words, usually to achieve greater clarity. This is an alternative way of referring to an author's ideas or arguments without using direct quotations from their text. Used properly, it has the added benefit of fitting more neatly into your own style of writing and allows you to demonstrate that you really do understand what the author is saying. However, you must ensure that you do not change the original meaning and you must still cite and reference your source of information.

> **Example**
>
> Harrison (2007, p. 48) clearly distinguishes between the historical growth of the larger European nation states and the roots of their languages and linguistic development, particularly during the fifteenth and sixteenth centuries. At this time, imperial goals and outward expansion were paramount for many of the countries, and the effects of spending on these activities often led to internal conflict.

Summarising

When you **summarise**, you provide a brief statement of the main points of an article, **web page**, chapter or book. This brief statement is known as a summary. It differs from paraphrasing in that it only lists the main topics or headings, with most of the detailed information being left out.

> **Example**
>
> Nevertheless, one important study (Harrison, 2007) looks closely at the historical and linguistic links between European races and cultures over the past five hundred years.

Section D
How to reference

Points to note

Students often find it difficult to differentiate between the terms **reference list** and **bibliography**.

The reference list is the detailed list of **references** cited in your assignment. It includes the full bibliographical information on sources, so that the reader can identify and locate the work/item.

A bibliography also provides a detailed list of references but includes background readings or other material you may have consulted, but not cited, in your text.

You should always check with your tutors whether they require you to include a reference list, a bibliography, or both (where you would provide a reference list and a separate bibliography of background readings). Either way, both are located at the end of your essay/piece of work. In the Harvard system, they are always arranged in alphabetical order by the author's surname/family name or, when there is no author, by title. For **web pages** where no author or title is apparent, the **URL** address should be used.

The fundamental points are that the reference links with your **citation** and includes enough information for the reader to be able to readily find the source again.

Example

> #### In-text citation
> In a recently published survey (Hill, Smith and Reid, 2010, p. 93), the authors argue that …
>
> #### Reference list
> Hill, P., Smith, R. and Reid, L. (2010) *Education in the 21st century.* London: Educational Research Press.

It is important that in your references you follow the format exactly for all sources, as shown in each example. This includes following the instructions consistently regarding the use of capital letters, typeface and punctuation.

Non-English naming conventions

Across the world there are several practices for naming individual people, including given name followed by family name (for example John Smith), family name followed by given name (for example Smith John), given name alone (for example John) and given name followed by father's name (for example John son of James). Within one country there may be several naming conventions employed by different ethnic groups.

When referencing names of authors in your work, you may be required to use a preferred naming convention. If in doubt, ask for advice from tutors or publishers, or copy the authors' expressions of their names. The principle followed in *Cite them right* (as with other authorities) is to place the family name first in the citation, followed by the initials of given names. The following examples show the complexity of this issue.

Arabic names

The given name precedes the family name. For example, Najīb Maḥfūz would be referenced as:

> **Example**
>
> Maḥfūz, N. (1980) *Afrāḥ al-qubbah* (Wedding song). al-Fajjālah: Maktabat Miṣr.

Yusuf al-Qaradawi would be referenced as:

> **Example**
>
> Qaradawi, Y. (2003) *The lawful and the prohibited in Islam*. London: Al-Birr Foundation.

Tariq Ramadan would be referenced as:

> **Example**
>
> Ramadan, T. (2008) *Radical reform: Islamic ethics and liberation*. Oxford: Oxford University Press.

When a man has completed the Hajj pilgrimage to Mecca, he may include Hajji in his name, for example Ragayah Hajji Mat Zin. Follow the order for the person's name given in the publication. For example, Ragayah Hajji Mat Zin would be referenced as:

> **Example**
>
> Ragayah, H.M.Z. (2008) *Corporate governance: role of independent non-executive directors*. Bangi: Institut Kajian Malaysia dan Antarabangsa, Universiti Kebangsaan Malaysia.

Burmese names

Individuals are usually referenced by the first element of their name. For example, Aung San Suu Kyi would be referenced as:

> **Example**
>
> Aung, S.S.K. (1991) *Freedom from fear and other writings*. London: Viking.

Chinese names

Traditionally, the family name is the first element of the individual's name and when citing use this first, as with Western names. For example, Hu Sen appears as Sen Hu in Western convention on the book title page, but in Chinese tradition would be referenced as:

> **Example**
>
> Hu, S. (2001) *Lecture notes on Chern-Simons-Witten theory*. Singapore and River Edge, NJ: World Scientific.

Zhang Boshu would be referenced as:

> **Example**
>
> Zhang, B. (1994) *Marxism and human sociobiology: the perspective of economic reforms in China*. Albany, NY: State University of New York Press.

If the author has adopted the convention of placing family name last, invert the elements as with Western names. For example, Sophia Tang would be referenced as:

> **Example**
>
> Tang, S. (2009) *Electronic consumer contracts in the conflict of laws*. Oxford: Hart Publishing.

Indian names

The given name precedes the family name. For example, Mohandas Gandhi would be referenced as:

> **Example**
>
> Gandhi, M.K. (1927) *An autobiography, or, the story of my experiments with truth*. Translated from the original in Gujarati by Mahadev Desa. Ahmedabad: Navajivan Press.

Japanese names

The family name precedes the given name. For example, Kenzaburō Ōe would be referenced as:

> **Example**
>
> Ōe, K. (1994) *The pinch runner memorandum*. Armonk, NY: M.E. Sharpe.

Note that many Japanese authors are known by given name then family name, for example Kenzaburō Ōe.

Malaysian names

Malay names may have a given name followed by a patronym or father's name, for example Nik Safiah Nik Ismail. Some names may have the family name followed by given names:

> **Example**
>
> Nik, S.N.I. (2010) *Soft skills: the what, the why, the how*. Bangi: Penerbit Universiti Kebangsaan Malaysia.

Portuguese names

In Portuguese naming conventions, individuals have a given name followed by their mother's family name and then their father's family name. Reference the father's family name first. For example, Armando Gonçalves Pereira would be referenced as:

> **Example**
>
> Pereira, A.G. (1949) *Algumas lições, conferências e discursos*. Lisbon: Editorial Império.

For names with particles (for example de), reference this after the initials of the given names. For example, André Luiz de Souza Filgueira would be referenced as:

> **Example**
>
> Souza Filgueira, A.L. de (2012) 'A utopia nacionalista de Manoel Bomfim', *Em Tempo de Histórias*, 20, pp. 153–163.

Spanish names

Traditionally, Spanish/Latin American individuals have a given name followed by their father's family name and then their mother's family name. When referencing these compound names, use the father's family name, following conventions for Western, Arabic and many other naming styles. For example, Pedro Vallina Martínez would be referenced as:

> **Example**
>
> Vallina Martínez, P. (1968) *Mis memorias*. México & Caracas: Tierra y Libertad.

Thai names

The given name is followed by the family name. For example, Piti Disyatat would be referenced as:

> **Example**
>
> Disyatat, P. (2011) 'The bank lending channel revisited', *Journal of Money, Credit and Banking*, 43(4), pp. 711–734.

Vietnamese names

Individuals are referenced by their family name, the first element of their names. For example, Võ Nguyên Giáp would be referenced as:

> **Example**
>
> Võ, N.G. (1975) *Unforgettable days*. Hanoi: Foreign Languages Publishing House.

Names with particles/prefixes

These are names that include, for example, d', de, de los, le, van and von.

It is difficult to provide definitive examples for all names with particles/prefixes, as each language has its own rules. As mentioned above, where possible copy the authors' own expressions of their names from the publication you are viewing and, if in any doubt, use the internet or library catalogues to confirm the details.

Elements that you may need to include in your references

Generally, the elements for inclusion for any source should be self-evident. Use the 'citation order' listed with the examples to help you identify the elements you should be looking for. When referencing some of the most commonly used sources try the following:

- *For books:* look on the title page or back of the title page (verso)
- *For printed journal articles:* look at the beginning of the article or at the table of contents of the journal issue
- *For electronic journal articles:* look at the top of the first page (before or after the article title)
- *For web pages:* look at the top and bottom of the first page, the logos and, for the URL, in the **address bar** at the top of your screen. You may find it helpful to right-click on the mouse and select 'Properties': this will often display the date the web page was last updated/modified.

Authors/editors

- When referencing four or more authors/editors in academic assignments you should either: reference the first name followed by *et al*. (meaning 'and others'), for example Harris, G.R. *et al*. (2016) …

  OR, if your **institution requires referencing of all named authors**:

  Harris, G.R., Miller, F., Baker, B., and Banks, M. (2016) …

- If you are writing for a publication you should follow the editor's guidelines, as you may be required to name all the authors in your reference list, regardless of the number, to ensure that each author's contribution is recognised
- Put the surname/family name first, followed by the initial(s) of given names, for example Hill, P.L.

NB For non-English names, see section above (p. 12)

- Some publications are written/produced by corporate bodies or organisations and you can use this name as the author, for example the National Trust. (See also the guidance given in 'Citing a corporate author' in Section B.) Note that the corporate author may also be the publisher
- If the publication is compiled by an editor or editors, signify this by using the abbreviation (ed.) or (eds), for example Parker, G. and Rouxeville, A. (eds)
- Do not use 'Anon.' if the author/editor is anonymous or no author/editor can be identified. Use the title of the work.

Year/date of publication

- Give the year of publication in round brackets after the author's/editor's name, for example Smith, L. (2014)
- If no date of publication can be identified, use (no date), for example Smith, L. (no date).

Title

- Use the title as given, together with the subtitle (if any), for example *Studying and working in Spain: a student guide*.

Edition

- Only include the edition number if it is not the first edition or if it is a revised edition (with or without a number, see next bullet). See also Section E1.1
- Edition is abbreviated to edn (to avoid confusion with the abbreviation ed. or eds for editor or editors), for example 3rd edn; or Rev. edn; or 4th rev. edn.

Place of publication and publisher

- Only required for printed books, reports etc.

- Separate the place of publication and the publisher with a colon, for example London: Initial Music Publishing
- If there is more than one place of publication, include only the most local
- For places of publication in the United States, add the abbreviated US state name (unless otherwise obvious), for example Cambridge, Mass.: Harvard University Press
- If a source is unpublished, please refer to Section E4.

Series/volumes (for books)

- Include series and individual volume number, if relevant, after the publisher, for example Oxford: Clio Press (World Bibliographical Series, 60).

Issue information (for journals, magazines and newspapers)

- When provided, you need to include the following information in the order:
  – volume number
  – issue/part number
  – date or season
  For example 87(3); or 19 July; or summer.

Page numbers

- Page numbers are only required in the reference list for chapters in books, and serial (journal/magazine/newspaper) articles
- The abbreviation p. is used for single pages and pp. for more than one, for example London: River Press, pp. 90–99. Note that page numbers are not elided (for example pp. 90–9) but written in full.

ISBNs

- Although ISBNs (International Standard Book Numbers) represent unique identifiers for books and eliminate confusion about editions and reprints, they are not commonly used in references.

Uniform/Universal Resource Locators (URLs)

- When using the URL address for web pages, you can shorten it, as long as the route remains clear
- Include the date you accessed the web page, for example (Accessed: 14 Feb 2015), or downloaded an ebook/music (Downloaded: 14 June 2015).

Digital Object Identifiers (DOIs)

- DOIs tag individual digital (online) sources. These sources can range from journal articles to conference papers and presentations. They include a number identifying the publisher, work and issue information. The following example shows how the DOI replaces the URL in the reference; note that, because the DOI is the permanent identifier for the source, it is not necessary to include an accessed date. In your reference lists DOI is always written in lower case, as in this example:

Example

Horch, E.P. and Zhou, J. (2012) 'Charge-coupled device speckle observations of binary stars', *Astronomical Journal*, 136, pp. 312–322. doi: 10.1088/0004-6256/136/1/312.

- You or your reader can locate a source by entering its DOI in an internet search engine.

Journal articles using article numbers and DOIs

- Some publishers now use article numbers instead of issue and page numbers
- The reference to the article includes the number of pages in the article

- Note that to see the page numbers, you may need to open the PDF version of the article. If this is not available, you may need to refer to the section number or even number the paragraphs and cite one of these for your reference, for example section 2.2, paragraph 3.

Example

Bond, J.W. (2008) 'On the electrical characteristics of latent finger mark corrosion of brass', *J. Phys. D: Appl. Phys*, 41, 125502 (10pp). doi:10.1088/0022-3727/41/12/125502.

Non-Roman scripts

You may need to reference sources that are not in Roman script as part of your work, for example Chinese and Arabic sources. It is recommended that you provide a translation of the title of the work in square brackets after the title in the original script.

You may also need to transliterate from the original language into Roman script. Chinese is transliterated into Pinyin and syllables are aggregated according to a Modern Chinese word dictionary. Arabic is transliterated according to the Library of Congress transliteration.

Example: Chinese Book with Chinese script

Pu, S. (1982) 聊斋志异 [*Strange stories of Liaozhai*]. Taiyuan: Shanxi Renmin Chubanshe.

Example: Chinese book with transliterated script in Pinyin

Pu, S. (1982) *Liao zhai zhi yi [Strange stories of Liaozhai]*. Taiyuan: Shanxi Renmin Chubanshe.

Example: Arabic books with Arabic script

Hussein, T. (1973)

المجموعة الكاملة لمؤلفات الدكتور طه حسين
[*The complete collection of Dr. Taha Hussein's works*]. Beirut: Dār al-Kitāb al-Lubnānī.

Example: Arabic book with Romanised script

Hussein, T. (1973) al-Majmūʻah al-kāmilah li-muʼallafāt al-Duktūr Tāhā Husayn [*The complete collection of Dr. Taha Hussein's works*]. Beirut: Dār al-Kitāb al-Lubnānī.

Sample text and reference list using Harvard (author-date) referencing style

NB This text makes extensive use of references for illustrative purposes only.

Text

A comparative study conducted by Bowman and Jenkins (2011), on properties built within the last twenty years and older houses, clearly illustrated the financial and environmental benefits of investing time and money in improving home insulation. A recent survey (Thermascan, 2012) and video (Norman, 2012) underlined that as much as a third of the heat generated in homes is lost through the walls or the roof as a result of poor insulation.

An article by Hallwood (2012) was fulsome in its praise of the work of organisations such as Tadea and the Energy Saving Trust in producing public information packs providing guidance on cavity wall and loft insulation. Further studies show that the amount of energy needed to heat our homes can have an ever-increasing impact on both the environment and family finances (BBC, 2010; Department of the Environment, 2011; Hampson and Carr, 2011). However, there is some criticism in the literature of the conflicting information regarding installation costs and the subsequent savings to be made (Kirkwood, Harper and Jones, 2011, pp. 49–58).

The relationship between climate change and energy use has been clearly emphasised by energy companies aiming to help potential customers 'supply their own energy with technologies such as solar panels and ground source heat pumps' (British Gas, 2012, p. 8). But huge challenges are posed by the conflict between expensive sustainable energy and family economic constraints, and these issues are examined in detail by Young (2012). What remains clear is that by finding ways in which we can significantly reduce our home running costs, we can simultaneously substantially reduce our carbon footprint (Strathearn, 2013).

Reference list

NB This list incorporates bubble captions to identify the type of source being referenced, which are used for illustrative purposes only.

BBC (2010) *Energy use and the environment.* Available at http://www.bbc.co.uk/energy (Accessed: 18 August 2012).

web page — see Section E8

Bowman, R. and Jenkins, S. (2011) 'Financial and environmental issues and comparisons in new and old build properties', in Harris, P. (ed.) *Studies on property improvements and environmental concerns in modern Britain.* London: Pinbury, pp. 124–145.

chapter in edited book — see Section E1.9

British Gas (2012) *A green light to save you more.* Eastbourne: British Gas.

company pamphlet/booklet — see Section E1.18

Department of the Environment (2011) *Energy and the environment in Britain today.* Available at: http://www.doe.gov.uk (Accessed: 12 January 2013).

online government report — see Section E13.2

Hallwood, L. (2012) 'The good work of sustainable energy organisations continues', *The Times*, 20 June, pp. 20–21.

electronic or print newspaper article — see Section E2.3

Hampson, P. and Carr, L. (2011) 'The impact of rising energy use on the environment: a five-year study', *Journal of Energy and Environmental Issues*, 53(5), pp. 214–231.

electronic or print journal article

see Section E2.1

Kirkwood, L., Harper, S. and Jones, T. (2011) *The DIY culture in Britain: costs for homes and the nation*. Available at: http://www.amazon.co.uk/kindle-ebooks (Downloaded: 8 September 2012).

signifies held on your own device

ebook downloaded onto edevice

see Section E1.3

Norman, L. (2012) *Heat loss in houses*. Available at http://www.youtube.com/watchheatlosshouseclm (Accessed: 18 March 2013).

YouTube video — see Section E21.9f

Strathearn, G. (2013) *Energy and environmental issues for the 21st century*. Basingstoke: Palgrave Macmillan.

print or electronic book

see Section E1

Thermascan (2012) *A report into costs and benefits relating to heat loss in homes*. Birmingham: Thermascan.

printed report — see Section E11

Young, L. (2012) *Sustaining our energy: challenges and conflicts*. Available at: http://books.google.com (Downloaded: 12 November 2012).

signifies held on your own device

ebook downloaded onto edevice

see Section E1.3

Top 10 tips

1. *Be aware*: if you don't already know, check with your tutor which referencing style you are expected to use

2. *Be positive*: used properly, references strengthen your writing, demonstrating that you have spent time researching and digesting material and produced your own opinions and arguments

3. *Be decisive* about the best way to cite your sources and how you balance your use of direct quotations, paraphrasing and summarising (read about these in Sections B and C)

4. *Be willing to ask for help*: library/learning resource staff offer support with referencing and academic skills

5. *Be organised*: prepare well and keep a record of all potentially useful sources as you find them

6. *Be prepared*: read Sections A to D before you begin your first assignment

7. *Be consistent*: once you have established the referencing style required, use it consistently throughout your piece of work

8. *Be patient*: make time and take your time to ensure that your referencing is accurate

9. *Be clear*: clarify the type of source you are referencing and check the appropriate section of *Cite them right* for examples

10. *Be thorough*: check through your work and your references before you submit your assignment, ensuring that your citations all match with a full reference and vice versa.

Checklist of what to include in your reference list for the most common information sources

	Author	Year of publication	Title of article/chapter	Title of publication	Issue information (volume/part numbers if available)	Place of publication	Publisher	Edition	Page number(s)	URL/DOI	Date accessed/ downloaded
Book	✓	✓		✓		✓	✓	✓			
Chapter from book	✓	✓	✓	✓		✓	✓	✓	✓		
Ebook	✓	✓		✓						URL if required	✓
Journal article (print and electronic)	✓	✓	✓	✓	✓				✓	DOI if required	
Web page	✓	✓		✓						✓	✓
Newspaper article (print and electronic)	✓	✓	✓	✓	✓				✓		

Section E
Harvard referencing style

NB Before looking at specific examples in this section, you should ensure that you have read Sections B, C and D.

E1 Books, including ebooks

The increasing availability of ebooks in identical form to print has rendered the distinction between the versions unnecessary. If the online source includes all the elements seen in print versions (that is, publication details, edition and page numbers), reference in the same way as print.

Only include the edition number if it is not the first or revised edition (see Section E1.1)

E1.1 Printed books

Citation order:
- Author/editor
- Year of publication (in round brackets)
- Title (in italics)
- Place of publication: publisher
- Series and volume number (where relevant)

Example: book with one author

In-text citation

According to Bell (2014, p. 23), the most important part of the research process is …

Reference list

Bell, J. (2014) *Doing your research project*. Maidenhead: Open University Press.

Example: book with two or three authors

In-text citation

Goddard and Barrett (2015) suggested …

Reference list

Goddard, J. and Barrett, S. (2015) *The health needs of young people leaving care*. Norwich: University of East Anglia, School of Social Work and Psychosocial Studies.

Example: book with four or more authors

In-text citation

This was proved by Young *et al.* (2015) …

Reference list

Young, H.D. *et al.* (2015) *Sears and Zemansky's university physics*. San Francisco, Calif.: Addison-Wesley.

OR, if your **institution requires referencing of all named authors**:

Young, H.D., Freedman, R.A., Sandin, T.R., and Ford, A.L. (2015) *Sears and Zemansky's university physics*. San Francisco, Calif.: Addison-Wesley.

Example: book with an editor

In-text citation

The formation of professions was examined in Prest (2014).

Reference list

Prest, W. (ed.) (2014) *The professions in early modern England*. London: Croom Helm.

Example: book with author(s) and editor(s)

In-text citation

Caroline (2007) points out …

Reference list

Caroline, N.L. (2007) *Nancy Caroline's emergency care in the streets*. Edited by Andrew N. Pollak, Bob Fellows and Mark Woolcock. Sudbury, Mass.: Jones and Bartlett.

In-text citation

The Percy tomb has been described as 'one of the masterpieces of medieval European art' (*Treasures of Britain and treasures of Ireland*, 1990, p. 84).

Reference list

Treasures of Britain and treasures of Ireland (1990) London: Reader's Digest Association Ltd.

For *second, later and revised editions* use the following:

Citation order:

- Author/editor
- Year of publication (in round brackets)
- Title (in italics)
- Edition (edition number and/or rev. edn.)
- Place of publication: publisher
- Series and volume number (where relevant)

(See also E1.2 Reprint and facsimile editions)

Example: later edition

In-text citation

The excellent study by Waugh (2015) …

Reference list

Waugh, D. (2015) *The new wider world*. 5th edn. Cheltenham: Nelson Thornes.

Examples: revised edition

In-text citation

The beautiful work by Moxon (2013) …

Reference list

Moxon, J. (2013) *The art of joinery*. Rev. edn. Fort Mitchell, Ky.: Lost Art Press.

In-text citation

Steinberg's wonderful analysis (2016, p. 45) …

Reference list

Steinberg, E.L. (2016) *Court music of Henry V.* 4th rev. edn. Oxford: Oxford University Press.

E1.2   Reprint and facsimile editions

For reprints and facsimile editions of older books, the year of the original publication (not the place of publication or publisher) is given, along with the full publication details of the reprint or facsimile.

Citation order:

- Author/editor
- Year of original publication (in round brackets)
- Title of book (in italics)
- Reprint or Facsimile of the …
- Place of reprint or facsimile publication: reprint or facsimile publisher
- Year of reprint or facsimile

Example: reprint

One of the first critics of obfuscation (David, 1968) …

Reference list

David, M. (1968) *Towards honesty in public relations*. Reprint, London: B.Y. Jove, 1990.

Example: facsimile

In-text citation

… his perfect blend of adventure, magic and fantasy (Tolkien, 1937).

Reference list

Tolkien, J.R.R. (1937) *The Hobbit*. Facsimile of the 1st edn. London: HarperCollins, 2016.

E1.3   Ebooks

When an ebook looks like a printed book, with publication details and pagination, you should reference as a printed book (see Section E1.1).

Citation order:

- Author/editor
- Year of publication (in round brackets)
- Title of book (in italics)
- Place of publication: publisher

Example

In-text citation

In their analysis, Hremiak and Hudson (2011, pp. 36–39) …

Reference list

Hremiak, A. and Hudson, T. (2011) *Understanding learning and teaching in secondary schools*. Harlow: Pearson Longman.

On some personal edevices specific ebook pagination details may not be available, so use the information you do have, such as loc, %, chapter/page/paragraph; for example (Richards, 2012, 67%), (Winters, 2011, ch. 4, p. 12).

When downloading ebooks, you may find it helpful to add a general statement at the end of your reference list informing your tutor that the texts are available on your edevice. You should also include the date that you downloaded them.

Citation order:

- Author/editor
- Year of publication (in round brackets)
- Title of book (in italics)
- Available at: URL
- (Downloaded: date)

Example

In-text citation

Arthur's argument with the council was interrupted by the Vogon Constructor Fleet (Adams, 1979, loc 876).

Reference list

Adams, D. (1979) *The hitchhiker's guide to the galaxy*. Available at: http://www. amazon.co.uk/kindle-ebooks (Downloaded: 29 January 2016).

E1.4   Audiobooks

Citation order:

- Author/editor
- Year of publication/release (in round brackets)
- Title of book (in italics)
- Narrated by (if required)
- Available at: URL
- (Downloaded: date)

Example

In-text citation

Covering 2000 years of medical history, Cunningham (2007) …

Reference list

Cunningham, A. (2007) *The making of modern medicine*. Available at: http://www.audiogo.com/uk/ (Downloaded: 18 March 2016).

E1.5 Historical books in online collections

If you are reading a scanned version of the printed book, complete with publication information and page numbers, reference in the same manner as the print book (see Section E1.1). Some early printed books do not have a publisher as they were privately printed. Record the information given in the book in your reference.

Citation order:

- Author/editor
- Year of publication (in round brackets)
- Title of publication (in italics)
- Place of publication and printing statement

> **Example**
>
> **In-text citation**
>
> Adam's measured plans (Adam, 1764) …
>
> **Reference list**
>
> Adam, R. (1764) *Ruins of the palace of the Emperor Diocletian at Spalatro in Dalmatia*. London: Printed for the author.

E1.6 Ancient texts

If citing an ancient text that existed before the invention of printing, reference it as a manuscript (see Section E26) or reference the published (and translated) edition you have read.

Citation order:

- Author
- Year of publication (in round brackets)
- Title of book (in italics)
- Translated by (if relevant)
- Edition (only include the edition number if it is not the first edition)
- Place of publication: publisher
- Series and volume number (where relevant)

> **Example**
>
> **In-text citation**
>
> The classic tale by Homer (1991) …
>
> **Reference list**
>
> Homor (1991) *The Iliad*. Translated by R. Fagles. Introduction and notes by B. Knox. London: Penguin Books.

E1.7 Translated books

Reference the translation you have read, not the original work.

Citation order:

- Author/editor
- Year of translated publication (in round brackets)
- Title of book (in italics)
- Translated by …
- Place of publication: publisher

> **Example**
>
> **In-text citation**
>
> Delibes, M. (2013) described childhood in a Spanish village.
>
> **Reference list**
>
> Delibes, M. (2013) *The path*. Translated by G. and R. Haycraft. London: Dolphin Books.

E1.8 Books in languages other than English

If referencing a book in its original language, give the title exactly as shown in the book.

Citation order:

- Author/editor
- Year of publication (in round brackets)
- Title of book (in italics)
- Place of publication: publisher

Example

In-text citation

Her depiction of middle-class lifestyles (Beauvoir, 1966) …

Reference list

Beauvoir, S. de (1966) *Les belles images*. Paris: Gallimard.

E1.9   Chapters/sections of edited books

Citation order:

- Author of the chapter/section (surname followed by initials)
- Year of publication (in round brackets)
- Title of chapter/section (in single quotation marks)
- 'in' plus author/editor of book
- Title of book (in italics)
- Place of publication: publisher
- Page reference

Example

In-text citation

The view proposed by Franklin (2012, p. 88) …

Reference list

Franklin, A.W. (2012) 'Management of the problem', in Smith, S.M. (ed.) *The maltreatment of children*. Lancaster: MTP, pp. 83–95.

E1.10   Multi-volume works

E1.10   a. Volumes or whole multi-volume works

Citation order:

- Author/editor
- Year of publication (in round brackets)
- Title of book (in italics)

- Volumes (in round brackets)
- Place of publication: publisher

Example

In-text citation

Butcher's (1961) guide …

Reference list

Butcher, R. (1961) *A new British flora* (4 vols.). London: Leonard Hill.

When citing a *single volume of a multi-volume work*, add the title of the relevant volume to your **reference list**.

Example

In-text citation

Part 3 of Butcher's work (1961) …

Reference list

Butcher, R. (1961) *A new British flora. Part 3: lycopodiaceae to salicaceae*. London: Leonard Hill.

E1.10   b. Chapters in multi-volume works

Citation order:

- Author of the chapter/section (surname followed by initials)
- Year of publication (in round brackets)
- Title of chapter/section (in single quotation marks)
- 'in' plus author/editor of book
- Title of book (in italics)
- Place of publication: publisher
- Page numbers of chapter/section

> **Example**
>
> **In-text citation**
>
> In analysing ports (Jackson, 2000) …
>
> **Reference list**
>
> Jackson, G. (2000) 'Ports 1700–1840', in Clark, P. (ed.) *Cambridge urban history of Britain: Vol. 2 1540–1840*. Cambridge: Cambridge University Press, pp. 705–731.

E1.10   c. Collected works

Citation order:

- Author/editor
- Year(s) of publication of collection (in round brackets)
- Title of book (in italics)
- Volumes (in round brackets)
- Place of publication: publisher

> **Example**
>
> **In-text citation**
>
> His collected works (Jung, 1989–1995) provide …
>
> **Reference list**
>
> Jung, C.G. (1989–1995) *Gesammelte Werke* (24 vols). Olten: Walter Verlag.

E1.11   Anthologies

Citation order:

- Editor/compiler of anthology (surname followed by initials)
- Year of publication (in round brackets)
- Title of book (in italics)
- Place of publication: publisher

> **Example**
>
> **In-text citation**
>
> In his collection of humorous poems, West (1989) …
>
> **Reference list**
>
> West, C. (compiler and illustrator) (1989) *The beginner's book of bad behaviour*. London: Beaver Books.

For *a line of a poem/prayer within an anthology*, use the following citation order:

- Author of the poem/prayer (surname followed by initials)
- Year of publication (in round brackets)
- Title of poem/prayer (in single quotation marks)
- 'in' plus author/editor/compiler of book
- Title of book (in italics)
- Place of publication: publisher
- Page reference

> **Example**
>
> **In-text citation**
>
> 'The lion made a sudden stop
> He let the dainty morsel drop' (Belloc, 1989, p. 89).
>
> **Reference list**
>
> Belloc, H. (1989) 'Jim', in West, C. (compiler and illustrator) *The beginner's book of bad behaviour*. London: Beaver Books, pp. 88–92.

E1.12   Lines within plays

Citation order:

- Author (surname followed by initials)
- Year of publication (in round brackets)
- Title (in italics)
- Edition information
- Place of publication: publisher
- Act.scene: line

Example

> **In-text citation**
>
> 'I prithee do not mock me fellow student'
> (Shakespeare, 1980, 1.2: 177).
>
> **Reference list**
>
> Shakespeare, W. (1980) *Hamlet*. Edited by
> Spencer, T.J.B. London: Penguin, 1.2:
> 177.

NB If referencing a *live performance*, see
Section E20.3.

E1.13 Bibliographies

Although print **bibliographies** have been
largely replaced by electronic sources for
current information, they may provide
commentary and highlight earlier writings.

Citation order:

- Author/editor
- Year of publication (in round brackets)
- Title (in italics)
- Edition (only include the edition number if it
  is not the first edition)
- Place of publication: publisher
- Series and volume number (where relevant)

Example

> **In-text citation**
>
> Ushpol (1958) noted the key research …
>
> **Reference list**
>
> Ushpol, R. (1958) *Select bibliography of
> South African autobiographies*. Cape
> Town: University of Cape Town, School of
> Librarianship.

E1.14 Reference books

In many cases, reference material (for
example dictionaries, encyclopedias, annuals
and bibliographies) does not have an obvious
author or editor, and is usually known and
therefore cited by its title.

Citation order:

- As for Section E1.1 (Printed books)

Example: with author

> **In-text citation**
>
> Beal (2008, p. 171) identified …
>
> **Reference list**
>
> Beal, P. (2008) 'Folio', *A dictionary of
> English manuscript terminology: 1450 to
> 2000*. Oxford: Oxford University Press.

Example: with no author

> **In-text citation**
>
> The definition (*Collins beginner's German
> dictionary*, 2014, p. 21) …
>
> **Reference list**
>
> *Collins beginner's German dictionary*
> (2014) New York, NY: Collins.

E1.15 Online reference books

As with other print sources, a growing
number of reference books are now available
as ebooks. As with other examples where
print and online versions exist, be careful to
reference the version you have used.
Sections E1.15a and E1.15b show how they
can vary.

E1.15 a. Printed books made available online

Reference these in the same manner as the
printed version.

Citation order:
As for Section E1.9 (Chapters/sections of
edited books)

E1.15 b. Books published in print and online, and updated at different times

In this case, the online version is updated regularly but the print version is not updated until a new edition is published, so the online version differs from the printed version. Replace publication details with:

- Available at: URL
- (Accessed: date)

E1.16 Sacred texts

E1.16 a. The Bible

There is a well-established system for citing references from the Bible in your text. This uses the book name, chapter and verse (not page number, as this will vary between printings). It also avoids stating authors, as the actual authorship of some books is unclear.

NB The publisher and publication date are not required.

Citation order:

- Book of the Bible
- Chapter: verse
- Holy Bible (not in italics)
- Version of the Holy Bible

> **Example**
>
> **In-text citation**
> The Beatitudes (Matthew 5: 3–12) …
>
> **Reference list**
> Matthew 5: 3–12, Holy Bible. New International Edition.

E1.16   b. The Torah

Citation order:
- Torah (not in italics)
- Book
- Chapter: verse

> **Example**
>
> **In-text citation**
> The reply (Shemot 3: 14) is the most profound …
>
> **Reference list**
> Torah. Shemot 3: 14.

E1.16   c. The Qur'an

Citation order:
- Qur'an (not in italics)
- Surah (or chapter): verse
- Year of publication (in round brackets)
- Translated by …
- Place of publication: publisher

> **Example**
>
> **In-text citation**
> 'And ease for me my task' (Qur'an 20: 26).
>
> **Reference list**
> Qur'an 20: 26 (2010) Translated by Abdel Haleem, M.A.S. Oxford: Oxford University Press.

E1.17   Atlases

NB See also Section E19.14 (Maps).

Citation order:
- As for Section E1.1 (Printed books)

> **Example**
>
> **In-text citation**
> As illustrated in the text (*The Times comprehensive atlas of the world*, 2011, p. 201) …
>
> **Reference list**
> *The Times comprehensive atlas of the world* (2011) 13th edn. London: Times Books.

E1.18   Pamphlets

Citation order:
- As for Section E1.1 (Printed books)

> **Example**
>
> **In-text citation**
> Bradley's pamphlet (1994) gave instructions in the use of …
>
> **Reference list**
> Bradley, M. (1994) *CD-ROMs: how to set up your workstation*. London: ASLIB.

E1.19   Exhibition catalogues

Citation order:
- Author of catalogue
- Year (in round brackets)
- Title of exhibition (in italics)
- Location and date(s) of exhibition
- [Exhibition catalogue]

Example

In-text citation

Urbach (2007, p. 8) noted the demands for reform …

Reference list

Urbach, P. (2007) *Reform! Reform! Reform!* Exhibition held at the Reform Club, London 2005–2006 and at Grey College, Durham University, March 2007 [Exhibition catalogue].

E2 Serials (journal/magazine/ newspaper articles – print and electronic)

It is worth pointing out that some serials have print and online equivalents (either with all details the same or with small variations, for example page numbers). Or, they may just be available online or in print editions. As always, you should reference the version that you are using. Students and tutors can access academic journal articles through password-protected institutional databases, but other readers may not have access to these. Therefore, as long as the serial reference provides enough bibliographic information for the article to be located by the reader, other elements (for example [Online], database title, including systematic review database titles such as *Cochrane Library* and **URL**) no longer need to be included. However, include the URL if you are using an article that is only available online (see the example below).

E2.1 Journal articles

Citation order:

- Author (surname followed by initials)
- Year of publication (in round brackets)
- Title of article (in single quotation marks)
- Title of journal (in italics – capitalise first letter of each word in title, except for linking words such as and, of, the, for)
- Issue information, that is, volume (unbracketed) and, where applicable, part number, month or season (all in round brackets)
- Page reference (if available)
- Available at: URL (if required) (Accessed: date) OR doi (if available)

Example: electronic or print or both

In-text citation

In their review of the literature (Norrie *et al.*, 2012) …

Reference list

Norrie, C. *et al.* (2012) 'Doing it differently? A review of literature on teaching reflective practice across health and social care professions', *Reflective Practice*, 13(4), pp. 565–578.

OR, if your **institution requires referencing of all named authors**:

Norrie, C., Hammond, J., D'Avray, L., Collington, V., and Fook, J. (2012) 'Doing it differently? A review of literature on teaching reflective practice across health and social care professions', *Reflective Practice*, 13(4), pp. 565–578.

Example: electronic article with doi

In-text citation

Shirazi's review article (2010) …

Reference list

Shirazi, T. (2010) 'Successful teaching placements in secondary schools: achieving QTS practical handbooks', *European Journal of Teacher Education*, 33(3), pp. 323–326. doi: 10.1080/02619761003602246.

Example: electronic article with no print equivalent (URL and no doi)

In-text citation

Barke and Mowl's excellent study (2016) …

Reference list

Barke, M. and Mowl, G. (2016) 'Málaga – a failed resort of the early twentieth century?', *Journal of Tourism History*, 2(3), pp. 187–212. Available at: http://www.tanfonline.com/full/1755182.2016 (Accessed: 23 April 2016).

If you are specifically referencing the *abstract* of a journal article, your **citation** would make this clear, for example: 'The abstract highlights … (Rodgers and Baker, 2013, p. 34).' Note that the reference would follow the same format as for a journal article because the page reference would take the reader to the abstract.

If referencing a *whole journal issue* use the following:

Citation order:

- Issue editor (if given)
- Year of publication (in round brackets)
- Title of issue (in single quotation marks)
- Title of journal (in italics – capitalise first letter of each word in title, except for linking words such as and, of, the, for)
- Issue information, that is, volume (unbracketed) and, where applicable, part number, month or season (all in round brackets)
- Available at: URL (if required) (Accessed: date) OR doi (if available)

Example: whole journal issue (electronic or print)

In-text citation

In the recent special issue (Harrison, 2016) …

Reference list

Harrison, P.R. (ed.) (2016) 'Alzheimer's – a transmissible disease?', *Trends in Medical Sciences*, 64(3).

NB For electronic whole journal issues with no print equivalent follow the example above, adding Available at: URL (Accessed: date) or doi.

For prepublication articles, see Section E7.3.

E2.2 Magazine articles

Citation order:

- Author (surname followed by initials)
- Year of publication (in round brackets)
- Title of article (in single quotation marks)
- Title of magazine (in italics – capitalise first letter of each word in title, except for linking words such as and, of, the, for)
- Issue information, that is, volume (unbracketed) and, where applicable, part number, month or season (all in round brackets)
- Page reference (if available)
- Available at: URL (if required) (Accessed: date) OR doi (if available)

Example: electronic or print article

In-text citation

Bletcher discussed body image (2012, p. 9) …

Reference list

Bletcher, K. (2012) 'Matters of the heart', *Heart Matters*, (August/September), pp. 9–11.

If referencing a *whole magazine issue* use the following:

Citation order:

- Issue editor (if given)
- Year of publication (in round brackets)
- Title of issue (in single quotation marks)
- Title of magazine (in italics – capitalise first letter of each word in title, except for linking words such as and, of, the, for)
- Issue information, that is, volume (unbracketed) and, where applicable, part number, month or season (all in round brackets)
- Available at: URL (if required) (Accessed: date) OR doi (if available)

NB For electronic whole magazine issues with no print equivalent follow the example above, adding Available at: URL (Accessed: date) or doi.

E2.3   Newspaper articles

Where the author (byline) of a newspaper article is identified, use the following citation order:

- Author/byline
- Year of publication (in round brackets)
- Title of article (in single quotation marks)
- Title of newspaper (in italics – capitalise first letter of each word in title, except for linking words such as and, of, the, for)
- Edition if required (in round brackets)
- Day and month
- Page reference (if available)
- Available at: URL (if required) (Accessed: date) OR doi (if available)

When referencing a *regional newspaper article*, include the edition to distinguish it from others with the same title.

Where no author (byline) is given, use the following citation order:

- Title of newspaper (in italics – capitalise first letter of each word in title, except for linking words such as and, of, the, for)
- Year of publication (in round brackets)
- Title of article (in single quotation marks)
- Day and month
- Page reference

Example: electronic or print article – no author

In-text citation

The article (*The Times*, 2012, p. 7) reported …

Reference list

The Times (2012) 'Bank accounts', 14 June, p. 7.

NB If you are specifically using the online version of a newspaper, which often varies from the print edition (for example no pagination), then you would reference it using the URL.

Example: electronic article with no print equivalent or one that varies from the print edition

In-text citation

US-led air strikes appeared to be imminent (Roberts and Ackerman, 2013).

Reference list

Roberts, D. and Ackerman, S. (2013) 'US draft resolution allows Obama 90 days for military action against Syria', *The Guardian*, 4 September. Available at: http://www.theguardian.com/world/2013/sep/04/syria-strikes-draftresolution-90-days (Accessed: 9 September 2015).

NB If you are citing several articles published in the same year, use a, b, c and so on after the year, for example *The Times* (2013a).

If you are referencing *letters* or *leading articles/editorials*, you would note this in your citations. When referencing a *section of a*

newspaper, where page numbering may well be the same as in the main newspaper, give the section as a subtitle.

Example: letter

In-text citation

In their letter, Fells *et al.* (2011, p. 23) …

Reference list

Fells, I. *et al.* (2011) 'Energise projects', *The Times*, 1 August, p. 23.

Example: leading article

In-text citation

In the leading article (*The Independent*, 2012, p. 28) …

Reference list

The Independent (2012) 'Grace in defeat', 27 January, p. 28.

Example: section

In-text citation

A recent article (*The Guardian*; G2, 2013, p. 14) …

Reference list

The Guardian: G2 (2013) 'Hope springs eternal', 24 July, p. 14.

If referencing a *whole newspaper issue* use the following.

Citation order:
- Title of newspaper (in italics – capitalise first letter of each word in title, except for linking words such as and, of, the, for)
- Year of publication (in round brackets)
- Edition if required (in round brackets)
- Day and month
- Available at: URL (if required) (Accessed: date)

Example: whole newspaper issue

In-text citation

Yesterday's copy of the newspaper (*The Independent*, 2016) …

Reference list

The Independent (2016) 17 April.

NB For electronic whole newspaper issues with no print equivalent follow the guidance given in E2.1 for electronic whole journal issues using the URL.

E3   Conferences

E3.1   Full conference proceedings

Citation order:

* Author/editor
* Year of publication (in round brackets)
* Title of conference: subtitle (in italics)
* Location and date of conference
* Place of publication: publisher

Example

In-text citation

The conference (Jones, 2015) …

Reference list

Jones, T. (ed.) (2015) *Small firms: adding the spark: the 23rd ISBA national small firms policy and research conference.* Robert Gordon University, Aberdeen, 15–17 November. Leeds: Institute for Small Business Affairs.

E3.2   Full conference proceedings published in journals

These are often published as special issues or journal supplements and are referenced as follows

Citation order:

* Title of conference, location and date (if included) (in single quotation marks)
* Year of journal publication (in round brackets)
* Title of journal (in italics – capitalise first letter of each word in title, except for linking words such as and, of, the, for)
* Issue information, that is, volume (unbracketed) and, where applicable, part number, month or season (all in round brackets)
* Available at: URL (if required) (Accessed: date) OR doi (if available)
  (you only need to include the URL or doi if the journal issue is only available online)

Example

In-text citation

The quality of all the papers ('Proceedings of the higher education technology conference', 2015) …

Reference list

'Proceedings of the higher education technology conference, University of Edinburgh, 23–25 March 2015' (2015) *Learning Online*, 27(4).

E3.3   Individual conference papers

Citation order:

* Author of paper
* Year of publication (in round brackets)
* Title of paper (in single quotation marks)
* Title of conference: subtitle (in italics)

- Location and date of conference
- Place of publication: publisher
- Page references for the paper

> **Example**
>
> **In-text citation**
>
> Cook (2014) highlighted examples ...
>
> **Reference list**
>
> Cook, D. (2014) 'Developing franchised business in Scotland', *Small firms: adding the spark: the 23rd ISBA national small firms' policy and research conference.* Robert Gordon University, Aberdeen, 15–17 November. Leeds: Institute for Small Business Affairs, pp. 127–136.

E3.4 Individual conference papers published in journals

Citation order:

- Author of paper
- Year of publication (in round brackets)
- Title of paper (in single quotation marks)
- from the Conference title, location and date (if included) (in round brackets)
- Title of journal (in italics)
- Issue information, that is, volume (unbracketed) and, where applicable, part number, month or season (all in round brackets)
- Page references for the paper
- Available at: URL (if required) (Accessed: date) OR doi (if available)
  (you only need to include the URL or doi if the journal paper is only available online)

> **Example**
>
> **In-text citation**
>
> The groundbreaking study (Pilsen, 2015) ...
>
> **Reference list**
>
> Pilsen, G. (2015) 'Online learning in higher education in China' (from the Proceedings of the higher education technology conference, University of Edinburgh, 23–25 March 2014), *Learning Online*, 27(4), pp. 42–57.

E3.5 Papers from conference proceedings published on the internet

Citation order:

- Author
- Year of publication (in round brackets)
- Title of paper (in single quotation marks)
- Title of conference: subtitle (in italics)
- Location and date of conference
- Page references for the paper (if available)
- Available at: URL (or doi if available)
- (Accessed: date) (not required when doi used)

> **Example**
>
> **In-text citation**
>
> A recent paper (Mendes and Romão, 2011) ...
>
> **Reference list**
>
> Mendes, L. and Romão, T. (2011) 'Children as teachers', *Proceedings of the 8th international conference on advances in computer entertainment technology*, Lisbon, Portugal, 8–11 November. doi: 10.1145/2071423.2071438.

E4 Unpublished and confidential information

Unpublished is generally understood as meaning 'not in the public domain'. This section includes a number of the most commonly used unpublished documents. However, other material can be found under headings that might be considered to be more relevant: for example Personal and virtual learning environments (Section E6), Visual sources (Section E19), Personal communications (Section E24) and Genealogical sources (Section E25).

E4.1 Theses

Citation order:

- Author
- Year of submission (in round brackets)
- Title of thesis (in italics)
- Degree statement
- Degree-awarding body

OR if viewed online:

- Available at: URL
- (Accessed: date)

Example

In-text citation

Research by Tregear (2013) and Parsons (2014) …

Reference list

Parsons, J.D. (2014) *Nutrition in contemporary diet*. PhD thesis. Durham University. Available at: http://etheses.dur.ac.uk/846 (Accessed: 14 August 2015).

Tregear, A.E.J. (2013) *Speciality regional foods in the UK: an investigation from the perspectives of marketing and social history*. Unpublished PhD thesis. Newcastle University.

E4.2 Tutors' handouts

NB For tutors' lecture notes in virtual learning environments, see Section E6.1.

You should always check with your tutor whether or not you are allowed to refer to course materials and your own work. It is more academically correct to refer to published sources.

Citation order:

- Tutor
- Year of distribution (in round brackets)
- Title of handout (in single quotation marks)
- Module code: module title (in italics)
- Institution
- Unpublished

Example

In-text citation

The tutor's handout (Hadley, 2015) …

Reference list

Hadley, S. (2015) 'Biomechanics: introductory readings', *BM289: Sport biomechanics*. University of Cumbria. Unpublished.

E4.3 Students' own work

Citation order:

- Student name
- Year of submission (in round brackets)
- Title of essay/assignment (in single quotation marks)
- Module code: module title (in italics)
- Institution
- Unpublished essay/assignment

Example

In-text citation

The topic of the essay (Sanders, 2015) …

Reference list

Sanders, M. (2015) 'An examination of the factors influencing air routes and the siting of international airports', *GEM1092: Geography and Environmental Management*. City University. Unpublished essay.

E4.4 Internal reports

NB For published reports, see Section E11.

Citation order:

- Author or organisation
- Year produced (in round brackets)
- Title of report (in italics)
- Internal report (including name of institution)
- Unpublished

Example

In-text citation

Recommendations in the report (Harris, 2013) …

Reference list

Harris, G. (2013) *Focus group recommendations*. Internal LGU report. Unpublished.

E4.5 Confidential information

In many cases you will need to anonymise the person or institution involved. In medical situations, for example, you may use terms such as 'Subject 1', 'Patient X' or 'Baby J' instead of real names; or 'Placement school', 'Placement hospital' or 'Placement agency' instead of actual institutions.

Citation order:

- Anonymised institution/agency (in square brackets)
- Year produced (in round brackets)
- Anonymised title (in italics) (use square brackets for the anonymised part)
- Location
- Anonymised producer (in square brackets)

Example

In-text citation

The records they produced (Placement hospital, 2012) …

Reference list

[Placement hospital] (2012) *[Placement hospital] examination criteria for elderly patients*. London: [Placement hospital].

If providing the town or city name is likely to identify a specific institution, you can simply insert the county, for example Lancashire: [Placement hospital].

Note that you may be asked by your tutor to supply them with the agency/employer name if there is any doubt about the authenticity of your reference.

NB See Section E19.6e for information relating to using and referencing medical images.

E5 Protocols, regulations and guidelines

These tend to relate to official procedures, rules and guidance from health, government and other corporate bodies.

For scientific and technical standards see Section E17.1.

Citation order:

- Author
- Year of publication (in round brackets)
- Title (in italics)

- Series or publication number (if given)
- Place of publication: publisher

OR if viewed online:
- Available at: URL
- Accessed: date

Example

In-text citation

The hospital's guideline (Great Ormond Street Hospital for Children, 2016) …

Reference list

Great Ormond Street Hospital for Children (2016) *Bone marrow biopsy*. Available at: http://www.gosh.nhs.uk/health-professionals/clinical-guidelines/bone-marrow-biopsy (Accessed: 18 February 2016).

E6 Personal and virtual learning environments, for example Blackboard, PebblePad and MOOCs

Personal learning environments/spaces (such as PebblePad) are often known as 'eportfolios' or 'webfolios'. They generally include a collection of electronic information (coursework, images, multimedia, hyperlinks and other electronic files) demonstrating the student's learning record and evidence of achievements. In many cases, eportfolios are now retained within university **virtual learning environments** (VLEs), which means that they are not easily accessible to anyone outside the VLE. External hosts like PebblePad can offer solutions to this problem, although issues relating to confidential information may persist (see Section E4.5).

In eportfolios, a multitude of different types of information may be referenced. However, the reference will always relate to the web page of the user's/student's work. For more specific examples, see: http://www.pebblepad.co.uk/examples.asp.

VLEs and collaboration suites such as Blackboard are used in further and higher education as stores for course documents and teaching materials, and for discussion between tutors and students and between students. You will need to distinguish what you are citing, for example a tutor's notes, a journal article, text extracted from a book and digitised for use in VLEs, or an item from a discussion board. Note in the examples below that the URL gives the access point to the VLE because a reader would need login details to locate the item being cited.

E6.1 Tutors' lecture notes

NB For unpublished tutors' handouts, see Section E4.2; for lecture notes/presentations available on the internet, see Section E23.1.

Citation order:
- Author or tutor
- Year of publication (in round brackets)
- Title of item (in single quotation marks)
- Module code: module title (in italics)
- Available at: URL of VLE
- (Accessed: date)

Example

In-text citation

The need for preparation (Hollis, 2015) …

Reference list

Hollis, K. (2015) 'Week 7: dissertation preparation materials'. *HIST 4271: Research methods for MA History*. Available at: http://duo.dur.ac.uk (Accessed: 21 November 2015).

E6.2 *PowerPoint* presentations

Citation order:

- Author or tutor
- Year of publication (in round brackets)
- Title of presentation (in single quotation marks)
- [*PowerPoint* presentation]
- Module code: module title (in italics)
- Available at: URL of VLE
- (Accessed: date)

> **Example**
>
> **In-text citation**
>
> The excellent presentation (Booth, 2014) ...
>
> **Reference list**
>
> Booth, L. (2014) 'History of radiography' [*PowerPoint* presentation]. *MISR4004: Patient care skills: an introduction to human sciences*. Available at: https://mylearning.cumbria.ac.uk (Accessed: 7 August 2015).

E6.3 Journal articles

For journal articles where you have all the required elements for the reader to track the article down you should simply cite and reference the article.

Citation order:

- Author
- Year of publication (in round brackets)
- Title of article (in single quotation marks)
- Title of journal (in italics)
- Volume, issue, page numbers

OR if journal is only available online add:

- Available at: URL (Accessed: date) or doi (if available)

> **Example**
>
> **In-text citation**
>
> Bright (2013, p. 262) believed ...
>
> **Reference list**
>
> Bright, M. (2013) 'The advance of learning', *Journal of Ideas*, 46(2), pp. 259–277.

E6.4 Learning support materials

Sometimes you will access, and need to reference, material from modules not produced by tutors, for example skills modules produced by learning support teams.

Citation order:

- Author
- Year of publication (in round brackets)
- Title of item (in single quotation marks)
- Title of support/skills module (in italics): subtitle (if required) (in italics)
- Available at: URL of VLE
- (Accessed: date)

> **Example**
>
> **In-text citation**
>
> ... and this module allows you to test your own skills (University of Cumbria, Library and Student Services, 2015).
>
> **Reference list**
>
> University of Cumbria, Library and Student Services (2015) 'Skills evaluation tools', *Skills@cumbria: assess your skills*. Available at: https://mylearning.cumbria.ac.uk (Accessed: 18 October 2015).

E6.5 Text extracts from books digitised for use in VLEs

Citation order:

- Author
- Year of publication of book (in round brackets)
- Extract title (in single quotation marks)
- 'in'
- Title of book (in italics)
- Place of publication: publisher (if available)
- Page numbers of extract
- Module code: module title (in italics)
- Available at: URL of VLE
- (Accessed: date)

Example

In-text citation

At least one author (Fenwick, 2014) …

Reference list

Fenwick, H. (2014) 'The Human Rights Act', in *Civil liberties and human rights*. London: Routledge Cavendish, pp. 157–298. *LAW 1032: Legal skills*. Available at: http://duo.dur.ac.uk (Accessed: 7 November 2015).

E6.6 Messages from course discussion boards

Citation order:

- Author
- Year of publication (in round brackets)
- Title of message (in single quotation marks)
- Title of discussion board (in italics)
- 'in'
- Module code: module title (in italics)
- Available at: URL of VLE
- (Accessed: date)

Example

In-text citation

It is advisable to check which referencing style is required (Thomas, 2015).

Reference list

Thomas, D. (2015) 'Word count and referencing style', *Frequently Asked Questions discussion board*, in *PHYS 2011: Housing Studies*. Available at: http://duo.dur.ac.uk (Accessed: 14 October 2015).

E6.7 MOOCs (Massive Online Open Courses)

Citation order:

- Producer
- Year of publication (in round brackets)
- Title of course (in italics)
- [MOOC]
- Available at: URL of MOOC
- (Accessed: date)

Example

In-text citation

… in relation to the University's MOOC (University of Bradford, 2016).

Reference list

University of Bradford (2016) *How to save energy* [MOOC]. Available at: https://www.bradford.ac.uk/mooccourses/energy26934/progress (Accessed: 10 July 2016).

E7 Digital repositories

Many academic and learned institutions maintain digital repositories of the research undertaken by their members and make digital copies (eprints) of book chapters, journal articles and conference papers available via the internet. Digital repositories are useful sources of new research and are often heavily cited in scientific literature.

If the book or article has already been published, reference it as the publication. Repositories can also be used by authors to present their articles to readers before traditional publication processes, such as **peer-review**, have been completed. Peer-review can take many months, by which time the value and opportunities raised by the new information may be lost. This form of rapid publication is common in the sciences, where early notice and discussion of new research is essential. If the articles are available before the item has been peer-reviewed, they are known as 'preprints'.

As with all internet-based sources, be clear what you are referencing. If it is a book, chapter or article that has already been published, reference it as you would the printed source, as in the book and conference paper examples below. However, if it is only available online use the URL (or DOI). If it is a prepublication article, conference, working paper or presentation that has not been peer-reviewed or formatted by publishers, or is a draft of a work that was published later, be clear that you are referencing the preprint, as this may be different from the later publication. Give the DOI or URL and accessed date and use [preprint] to highlight to your reader that you have read the preprint, not the final approved article.

E7.1 Books in digital repositories

Reference books and journal articles in repositories as you would for print versions (unless they are only available online, in which case use the URL or DOI).

Examples

In-text citation

Previous PhD candidates provided useful advice (Cook and Crang, 2013).

Reference list

Cook, I. and Crang, M. (2013) *Doing ethnographies*. Norwich: Geobooks.

In-text citation

The research process highlighted … (James and Phelps, 2014).

Reference list

James, P. R. and Phelps, J. (2014) *The dynamic research process*. Available at: http://archivos.com/18736 (Accessed: 23 November 2015).

E7.2 Conference papers in digital repositories

If the conference paper is only available online give the URL or DOI.

Citation order:
- Author
- Year of publication (in round brackets)
- Title of paper (in single quotation marks)
- Title of conference: subtitle (in italics)
- Organisation or company (if stated)
- Location and date of conference
- Available at: URL (if required) (Accessed: date) OR doi (if available)

E7.3 Prepublication journal articles online or in digital repositories

Citation order:

- Author
- Year (in round brackets)
- Title of article (in single quotation marks)
- To be published in (if this is stated)
- Title of journal (in italics and capitalise first letter of each word in title, except for linking words such as and, of, the, for)
- Volume and issue numbers (if stated)
- [Preprint]
- Available at: URL (Accessed: date) OR doi (if available)

E8 The internet

When referencing information you have retrieved from the internet, *you must distinguish what you are referring to*. The internet is made up of journal articles, organisation internet sites, personal internet sites, government publications, images, company data, presentations – a vast range of material. Examples of how to reference individual sources, such as journal articles, ebooks and images, are given with the entries for those sources. In this section you will find examples of how to cite and reference internet sites or **web pages** produced by individuals and organisations.

The nature of what you are referring to will govern how you cite or reference it. You should aim to provide sufficient information for a reader to be able to locate your information source. As material on the internet can be removed or changed, you should also note the date when you accessed/viewed the information – it might not be there in a few months' time.

Remember to evaluate all internet information for accuracy, authority, currency, coverage and objectivity. The ability to publish information on the internet bears no relation to the author's academic abilities.

The defining element in referencing a web page is its Uniform Resource Locator, or URL. This should be included in your reference list, but *do not include the URL in your **in-text citation**, unless this is the only piece of information you have.*

E8.1 Web pages with individual authors

Citation order:
- Author
- Year that the site was published/last updated (in round brackets)
- Title of web page (in italics)
- Available at: URL
- (Accessed: date)

Example

In-text citation

Burton (2012) provided information for the visit.

Reference list

Burton, P.A. (2012) *Castles of Spain*. Available at: http://www.castlesofspain. co.uk/ (Accessed: 14 October 2015).

E8.2 Web pages with organisations as authors

Example

In-text citation

After identifying symptoms (National Health Service, 2015) …

Reference list

National Health Service (2015) *Check your symptoms*. Available at: http://www. nhsdirect.nhs.uk/checksymptoms (Accessed: 17 October 2015).

E8.3 Web pages with no authors

Use the title of the web page.

Example

In-text citation

llustrations of the houses can be found online (*Palladio's Italian villas*, 2005).

Reference list

Palladio's Italian villas (2005) Available at: http://www.boglewood.com/palladio/ (Accessed: 23 August 2015).

E8.4 Web pages with no authors or titles

If no author or title can be identified, you should use the web page's URL. It may be possible to shorten a very long URL, as long as the route remains clear, but it may be necessary to give the full URL even in your citation. If a web page has no author or title, you might question whether or not it is suitable for academic work.

Example

In-text citation

Video files may need to be compressed (http://www.newmediarepublic.com/ dvideo/compression.html, 2014).

Reference list

http://www.newmediarepublic.com/ dvideo/compression.html (2014) (Accessed: 14 July 2015).

E8.5 Web pages with no dates

If the web page has no obvious date of publication/revision, use the Author (no date) and the date you accessed the page. You might question how useful undated information is to your research as it may be out of date.

You should not use web pages for academic work which have no obvious author, title or date.

E8.6 Blogs/vlogs

Blogs (weblogs) and vlogs (video logs) are produced by individuals and organisations to provide updates on issues of interest or concern. Be aware that, because blogs/vlogs are someone's opinions, they may not provide objective, reasoned discussion of an issue. Use blogs/vlogs in conjunction with reputable sources. Note that, due to the informality of the internet, many authors give first names or aliases. Use the name they have used in your reference.

Citation order:

* Author of message
* Year that the site was published/last updated (in round brackets)
* Title of message (in single quotation marks)
* Title of internet site (in italics)
* Day/month of posted message
* Available at: URL
* (Accessed: date)

NB For the social networking site *Twitter*, see Section E8.8.

E8.7 Wikis

Wikis are collaborative websites in which several (usually unidentified) authors can add and edit the information presented. What you read today may have changed by tomorrow. There have also been instances of false information being presented, although wiki editors try to ensure that the information is authentic. If you are going to use information from a wiki, *make sure that it is thoroughly referenced*. As with other websites, if no authors or references are given, the information is unlikely to be suitable for academic work. Evaluate wiki information against sources of proven academic quality such as books and journal articles.

Citation order:

* Title of article (in single quotation marks)
* Year that the entry was published/last updated (in round brackets)
* Title of wiki site (in italics)
* Available at: URL
* (Accessed: date)

> **Example**
>
> **In-text citation**
>
> Telford introduced new techniques of bridge construction ('Thomas Telford', 2014).
>
> **Reference list**
>
> 'Thomas Telford' (2014) *Wikipedia*. Available at: http://en.wikipedia.org/wiki/Thomas_Telford (Accessed: 11 September 2015).

E8.8   Social networking websites

Note that, because these sites require registration and then acceptance by other members, it is suggested that the main web address be used. You may wish to include a copy of the member-to-member discussion you are referring to as an appendix to your work, so that readers without access to the original can read it.

Hashtags # are a common sight now on *Twitter*, *Facebook*, *Instagram*, *Google+*, *Flickr*, *Tumblr*, *Pinterest* and other platforms, and you may wonder how to cite and reference them. The answer is that you do not. This is because, just like your research on a database, finding and searching with the right hashtag is part of your research methodology. So, you can simply describe it in your text: for example, 'During the recent migrant crisis in Europe I searched *Twitter* and *Instagram* for the hashtags #refugees, #migrants and #asylumseekers appearing between September 1, 2015 and October 15, 2015'. Your reader can then try to replicate the search if they wish to follow your evidence. To reference any tweets, posts or photographs that you find on social networking sites you should follow the relevant examples.

E8.8   a. *Facebook*

Citation order:

- Author (if available; if not, use title)
- Year that the page was published/last updated (in round brackets)
- Title of page (in italics)
- [*Facebook*]
- Day/month of posted message
- Available at: URL
- (Accessed: date)

> **Example**
>
> **In-text citation**
>
> The campaign had over 7,000 members in less than one week (*Tynemouth outdoor pool*, 2015).
>
> **Reference list**
>
> *Tynemouth outdoor pool* (2015) [*Facebook*] 29 August. Available at: https://www.facebook.com (Accessed: 31 August 2015).

NB For images seen through social media sites, see Section E19.6c.

E8.8   b. *Twitter*

Citation order:

- Author
- Year tweet posted (in round brackets)
- [*Twitter*]
- Day/month tweet posted
- Available at: URL
- (Accessed: date)

Example

In-text citation

One celebrity (Fry, 2015) tweeted messages of support.

Reference list

Fry, S. (2015) [*Twitter*] 13 January. Available at: https://twitter.com/stephenfry (Accessed: 18 December 2015).

E9 CD-ROMs or DVD-ROMs

Citation order:

- Title of publication (in italics)
- Year of publication (in round brackets)
- [CD-ROM] or [DVD-ROM]
- Producer (where identifiable)
- Available: publisher/distributor

Example

In-text citation

The student made extensive use of an authoritative source (*World development indicators*, 2002) …

Reference list

World development indicators (2002) [CD-ROM]. The World Bank Group. Available: SilverPlatter.

E10 Computer/video games, computer programs and mobile apps

E10.1 Computer/video games

These may be purchased games played on platforms such as *PlayStation*, *Xbox* and smartphones, or downloaded directly from the internet.

Citation order:

- Company/individual developer
- Release year (in round brackets)

- Title of game (in italics and capitalise initial letters – include edition if relevant)
- [Video game]
- Publisher

OR if downloaded from the internet add:

- Available at: URL
- (Downloaded: date)

Examples

In-text citation

Two of the most popular online games *FIFA 16 Deluxe Edition* (EA, 2015) and *Halo 5: Guardians* (343 Industries, 2015) …

Reference list

343 Industries (2015) *Halo 5: Guardians – Digital Deluxe Edition* [Video game]. Microsoft Studios. Available at: http://www.xbox.com/en-gb/Search?q=Halo+5 (Downloaded: 28 March 2016).

EA (2015) *FIFA 16 Deluxe Edition* [Video game]. Electronic Arts.

E10.2 Computer programs

Citation order:

- Author (if given)
- Date – if given (in round brackets)
- Title of program (in italics and capitalise initial letters)
- Version (in round brackets)
- [Computer program]
- Availability, that is, distributor, address, order number (if given)

OR if downloaded from the internet:

- Available at: URL
- (Downloaded: date)

> **Example**
>
> **In-text citation**
>
> *Camtasia Studio* (TechSmith, 2012) can be used to record tutorials.
>
> **Reference list**
>
> TechSmith Corporation (2012) *Camtasia Studio* (Version 3) [Computer program]. Available at: http://www.techsmith.com/download.html (Downloaded: 21 June 2015).

E10.3   Mobile apps

Use the name of the producer of the app if available. If not use the title of the app as the first element.

Citation order:

- Producer (if given)
- Year of release/update (in round brackets)
- Title of app (in italics and capitalise initial letters)
- Edition (if given)
- Version number – if given (in round brackets)
- [Mobile app]
- Available at: app store name
- (Downloaded: date)

> **Example**
>
> **In-text citation**
>
> *RealPlayer Cloud* (RealNetworks Inc., 2013) allows extra storage space to move, watch and store your videos.
>
> **Reference list**
>
> RealNetworks Inc. (2013) *RealPlayer Cloud.* Kindle & Fire Phone edition. (Version 1.6.28) [Mobile app]. Available at: Amazon Appstore (Downloaded: 6 February 2016).

E11   Reports

NB For unpublished internal reports, see Section E4.4.

Citation order:

- Author or organisation
- Year of publication (in round brackets)
- Title of report (in italics)
- Place of publication: publisher

OR if accessed on the internet:

- Available at: URL
- (Accessed: date)

E11.1   Research reports

> **Example**
>
> **In-text citation**
>
> The minimum cost of living in Britain is £13,400 (Bradshaw *et al.*, 2013, p. 32).
>
> **Reference list**
>
> Bradshaw, J. *et al.* (2013) *A minimum income standard for Britain: what people think*. Available at: http://www.jrf.org.uk/sites/files/jrf/2226-income-poverty-standards.pdf (Accessed: 3 July 2015).

E11.2   Company annual reports

> **Example**
>
> **In-text citation**
>
> The company's profits expanded (BSkyB Ltd, 2014) …
>
> **Reference list**
>
> BSkyB Ltd. (2014) *Annual report 2014*. Available at: http://annualreview2014sky.com/_assets/downloads/PDF/SKYAnnRep2011/Full_Annual_Report_2014.pdf (Accessed: 8 January 2016).

E11.3 Market research reports from online databases

Example

In-text citation

Mintel Oxygen (2014) noted problems in the market …

Reference list

Mintel Oxygen (2014) 'Car insurance UK'. Available at: http://academic.mintel.com (Accessed: 5 January 2016).

NB The section of the report collection is given in single quotation marks.

E11.4 Financial reports from online databases

Citation order:

- Publishing organisation
- Year of publication/last updated (in round brackets)
- Title of extract (in single quotation marks)
- Available at: URL
- (Accessed: date)

Example

In-text citation

BT's profit margin rose by over 2 per cent in the financial year 2014–2015 (Bureau van Dijk, 2015).

Reference list

Bureau van Dijk (2015) 'BT Group plc company report'. Available at: http://fame.bvdep.com (Accessed: 5 October 2015).

E12 United Kingdom legal sources using the Harvard (author-date) style

In this edition of *Cite them right* we give examples for citing legal sources in author-date (Harvard) format. In previous editions we employed the referencing systems used in many UK law schools, but many other disciplines use legal sources in their research and do not apply the same conventions for publication abbreviations and punctuation as the law schools. Providing examples for citing legal sources in author-date (Harvard) format will ensure that scholars in other disciplines, who already use author-date referencing for non-legal sources, and their readers, can identify legal sources using methods which are familiar to them.

The author-date format uses the elements of references common to other sources as the in-text and reference list documentation: speakers recorded in *Hansard* are treated as authors; law reports are treated as journal articles with the case name used as the article title.

UK legislation is available on *BAILII* (http://www.bailii.org/), *Legislation.gov.uk* (http://www.legislation.gov.uk/) and subscription services including *LexisLibrary* and *Westlaw*.

E12.1 Papers: House of Commons and House of Lords

Citation order:

- Parliament. House of …
- Year of publication (in round brackets)
- Title (in italics)
- Paper number (in round brackets). For House of Lords papers, the paper number is also in round brackets to distinguish it from identical House of Commons paper numbers (see examples below)
- Place of publication: publisher

E12.2 Official records: House of Commons and House of Lords

E12.2 a. *Hansard*

Hansard is the official record of debates, speeches, oral and written answers/statements, petitions and Westminster Hall discussions in the Houses of the UK Parliament. A fully searchable version of *Hansard* from 1988 for the Commons and from 1995 for the Lords is available online at http://www.parliament.uk/business/publications/hansard/. Historical records for *Hansard* from 1803 to 2005 are available online at http://hansard.millbanksystems.com/.

Citation order:

- Name of speaker/author
- Year of publication (in round brackets)
- Subject of debate or speech (in single quotation marks)
- Hansard: Name of House of Parliament (in italics)
- Debates/written statement/Westminster Hall or petitions (in italics)
- Day and month
- Volume number, column number or page number
- Available at: URL
- (Accessed: date)

E12.2 b. *Written questions and answers* and *Written ministerial statements*

Before September 2014, written questions and answers and written statements were recorded in *Hansard*.

Citation order:

- Name of author
- Year of publication (in round brackets)
- Subject of question, answer or statement (in single quotation marks)
- Hansard: Name of House of Parliament (in italics)
- Debates/written statement/Westminster Hall or petitions (in italics)
- Day and month
- Volume number, column number or page number
- Available at: URL
- (Accessed: date)

Since 12 September 2014, written questions and answers have been published in the *Written questions and answers* database (http://www.parliament.uk/business/ publications/written-questions-answers-statements/written-questions-answers/) instead of *Hansard*. This means that the column reference is no longer used. Questions and answers in the database are given a number to include in their citation.

Citation order:

- Name of author
- Year of publication (in round brackets)
- Subject of question, answer or statement (in single quotation marks)
- Parliament: written questions and written answers (in italics)
- Day and month
- Question number
- Available at: URL
- (Accessed: date)

E12.3 Bills: House of Commons and House of Lords

Citation order:

- Title (in italics)
- Year of publication (in round brackets)
- Parliament: House of Commons or Lords
- Bill number
- Place of publication: publisher

E12.4 UK statutes (Acts of Parliament)

Before 1963 an Act was cited according to the regnal year (that is, the number of years since the monarch's accession). You may see references to legislation in this format in early publications, for example *Act of Supremacy 1534* (26 Hen 8 c1). However, for all Acts (including pre-1963) you should use the short title of the Act, with the year in which it was enacted. Most Acts and parts of Acts are now available as PDFs or web pages to be viewed online, so reference the website where you located the Act.

NB As the date appears in the title of the Acts, there is no need to repeat the date in round brackets after the title.

If you are referencing documents from more than one country (jurisdiction), include the country (jurisdiction) in round brackets after the title of the documentation (see examples in Section E15).

Citation order:
- Title of Act including year and chapter number (in italics)
- Country/jurisdiction (only if referencing more than one country's legislation)
- Available at: URL
- (Accessed: date)

Example: whole Act

> **In-text citation**
>
> Recent social care legislation (*Health and Social Care Act 2012*) ...
>
> **Reference list**
>
> *Health and Social Care Act 2012, c. 7.* Available at: http://www.legislation.gov.uk/ukpga/2012/7/contents/enacted (Accessed: 17 September 2015).
>
> OR if you use the PDF version:
>
> Available at: http://www.legislation.gov.uk/ukpga/2012/7/pdfs/ukpga_20120007_en.pdf (Accessed: 17 September 2015).

Example: section of an Act

> **In-text citation**
>
> As defined in section 10(2) of the Act (*Children Act 2004*) ...
>
> **Reference list**
>
> *Children Act 2004, c. 31.* Available at: http://www.legislation.gov.uk/ukpga/2004/31/contents (Accessed: 17 September 2015).

E12.5 Statutory Instruments (SIs)

Citation order:
- Name/title including year (in italics)
- SI year and number (in round brackets)
- Available at: URL
- (Accessed: date)

Example

> **In-text citation**
>
> Referring to the *General Dental Council (Constitution) (Amendment) Order 2012* ...
>
> **Reference list**
>
> *General Dental Council (Constitution) (Amendment) Order 2012* (SI 2012/1655). Available at: http://www.legislation.gov.uk/uksi/2012/1655/contents/made (Accessed: 17 September 2015).

E12.6 Legislation from UK devolved legislatures

NB Legislation from UK devolved legislatures is available online at http://www.legislation.gov.uk.

E12.6 a. Acts of the Scottish Parliament

For Acts of the post-devolution Scottish Parliament, replace the chapter number with 'asp' (meaning Act of the Scottish Parliament).

Citation order:

- Title of Act including year (in italics)
- asp number (in round brackets)
- Available at: URL
- (Accessed: date)

Example

`In-text citation`

In the legislation (*Budget (Scotland) Act 2015*) ...

`Reference list`

Budget (Scotland) Act 2015 (asp 2). Available at: http://www.legislation.gov.uk/asp/2015/2/contents (Accessed: 17 September 2015).

E12.6   b. Scottish Statutory Instruments (SSIs)

Citation order:

- Title of SSI including year (in italics)
- SSI number
- Available at: URL
- (Accessed: date)

Example

`In-text citation`

In the SSI of 2005 (*Tuberculosis (Scotland) Order 2005*) ...

`Reference list`

Tuberculosis (Scotland) Order 2005, SSI 2005/434. Available at: http://www.legislation.gov.uk/ssi/2005/434/contents/made (Accessed: 17 September 2015).

E12.6   c. Acts of the Northern Ireland Assembly

Citation order:

- Title of Act (Northern Ireland) including year (in italics)
- Available at: URL
- (Accessed: date)

Example

`In-text citation`

... which was discussed in the legislation (*Pensions Act (Northern Ireland) 2015*).

`Reference list`

Pensions Act (Northern Ireland) 2015. Available at: http://www.legislation.gov.uk/nia/2015/5/contents (Accessed: 17 September 2015).

E12.6   d. Statutory Rules of Northern Ireland

The Northern Ireland Assembly may pass Statutory Instruments. These are called Statutory Rules of Northern Ireland.

Citation order:

- Title of Rule (Northern Ireland) including year (in italics)
- SR year/number
- Available at: URL
- (Accessed: date)

Example

`In-text citation`

The rules relating to flavourings (*Smoke Flavourings Regulations (Northern Ireland) 2005*) ...

`Reference list`

Smoke Flavourings Regulations (Northern Ireland) 2005, SR 2005/76. Available at: http://www.legislation.gov.uk/nisr/2005/76/contents/made (Accessed: 17 September 2015).

E12.6   e. National Assembly for Wales legislation

The National Assembly for Wales may pass Assembly Measures (nawm), which are primary legislation but are subordinate to UK statutes.

Citation order:

- Title of Assembly Measure including year (in italics)
- (nawm number)
- Available at: URL
- (Accessed: date)

Example

In-text citation

The 2008 Measure (*NHS Redress (Wales) Measure 2008*) ...

Reference list

NHS Redress (Wales) Measure 2008 (nawm 1). Available at: http://www. legislation.gov.uk/mwa/2008/1/2008-07-09 (Accessed: 17 September 2015).

The National Assembly for Wales may also pass Statutory Instruments. As well as the SI number and year, Welsh Statutory Instruments have a W. number.

Citation order:

- Title of Order (Wales) including year (in italics)
- Welsh Statutory Instrument year/SI number (W. number)
- Available at: URL
- (Accessed: date)

Example

In-text citation

The Welsh Statutory Instrument (*The Bluetongue (Wales) Order 2003*) ...

Reference list

The Bluetongue (Wales) Order 2003 Welsh Statutory Instrument 2003/326 (W.47). Available at: http://www.legislation.gov.uk/wsi/2003/326/contents/made (Accessed: 17 September 2015).

E12.7 Law Commission reports and consultation papers

Citation order:

- Law Commission
- Year of publication (in round brackets)
- Title of report or consultation paper (in italics)
- Number of report or consultation paper, Command Paper number (if given) (in round brackets)
- Place of publication: publisher

OR if viewed online:

- Available at: URL
- (Accessed: date)

Examples

In-text citation

The report (Law Commission, 2001) recommended that retrial after acquittal should be permitted in cases of murder, if new evidence became available.

Reference list

Law Commission (2001) *Double Jeopardy and Prosecution Appeals.* (Law Com No 267, Cm 5048). London: The Stationery Office.

OR

Law Commission (2001) *Double Jeopardy and Prosecution Appeals.* (Law Com No 267, Cm 5048). Available at: http://lawcommission.justice.gov.uk/areas/doublejeopardy.htm (Accessed: 17 September 2015).

E12.8 Command Papers including Green and White Papers

Citation order:

- Department
- Year of publication (in round brackets)

- Title of report or consultation paper (in italics)
- Command Paper number (in round brackets)
- Place of publication: publisher

OR if viewed online:

- Available at: URL
- (Accessed: date)

Examples

In-text citation

In her essay she cited proposals on the Minimum Wage (Department for Children, Schools and Families, 2010; Department for Business, Innovation & Skills, 2015).

Reference list

Department for Business, Innovation & Skills (2015) *Regulations implementing the National Minimum Wage – a report on the Apprentice Rate* (Cm 9061). Available at: https://www.gov.uk/government/publications/national-minimum-wage-report-on-the-2015-apprentice-rate (Accessed: 17 September 2015).

Department for Children, Schools and Families (2010) *Support for all* (Cm 7787). London: The Stationery Office.

E12.9   Law reports (cases)

Citation order:

- Name of case (in single quotation marks)
- Year (in round brackets)
- Title of law report (in italics)
- Volume number
- Page numbers

Example

In-text citation

The earlier case ('R v. Edward (John)', 1991) …

Reference list

'R v. Edward (John)' (1991) *Weekly Law Reports*, 1, pp. 207–208.

Neutral citations

From 2002 cases have been given a neutral citation that identifies the case without referring to the printed law report series in which the case was published. This helps to identify the case online, for example through the freely available transcripts of the British and Irish Legal Information Institute (www.bailii.org) and databases including *Westlaw* and *LexisLibrary*. If you are using the neutral citation, also provide the publication in which the case was reported or the database or website that you used.

Citation order:

- Name of parties involved in case (in single quotation marks)
- Year (in round brackets)
- Court and case no.
- Database or website (in italics)
- [Online]
- Available at: URL
- (Accessed: date)

E12.10   Inquiries

Public and independent inquiries may be published by order of Parliament, and if so are given a Parliamentary or Command Paper number.

Citation order:

- Author
- Year of publication (in round brackets)
- Title of inquiry (in italics)
- Parliamentary or Command Paper number (in round brackets)
- Place of publication: publisher

OR if viewed online:

- Available at: URL
- (Accessed: date)

E13 European Union (EU) legal sources

Legal documents from the EU include legislation, directives, decisions and regulations. The most authoritative source is the *Official Journal of the European Union*.

E13.1 EU legislation

Citation order:

- Legislation title (in italics)
- Year (in round brackets)
- Official Journal (in italics)
- Series initial issue
- Page numbers

> **Example**
>
> **In-text citation**
>
> All signatories to the Treaty (*Consolidated Version of the Treaty on European Union*, 2008) …
>
> **Reference list**
>
> *Consolidated Version of the Treaty on European Union* (2008) *Official Journal* C 115, 9 May, pp.13–45.

E13.2 EU directives, decisions and regulations

Citation order:

- Legislation type (in single quotation marks)
- Number and title (in single quotation marks)
- Year (in round brackets)
- Official Journal (OJ) series (in italics)
- Issue
- Page numbers

OR

- Available at: URL
- (Accessed: date)

Examples

In-text citation

The minister highlighted the terms of 'Council directive 2008/52/EC' (2008), 'Council regulation (EU) 2015/760' (2015) and 'DS Smith/Duropack' (2015) …

Reference list

Directives
'Council directive 2008/52/EC on certain aspects of mediation in civil and commercial matters' (2008) *Official Journal* L136, p. 3.

Regulations
'Council regulation (EU) 2015/760 on European long-term investment funds' (2015) *Official Journal* L123, p. 98.

Commission decisions are cited as cases
'Case M.7558 – DS Smith/Duropack' (2015) Commission decision. *Eur-Lex*. Available at: http://ec.europa.eu/competition/mergers/cases/decisions/m7558_20150521_20310_4308239_EN.pdf (Accessed: 27 September 2015).

E13.3 Judgements of the European Court of Justice (ECJ) and General Court (GC)

Citation order:

- Case name (in single quotation marks)
- Year (in round brackets)
- Case number
- Publication title (in italics)
- Section, page numbers

Example

In-text citation

Consideration of the Swedish view ('Commission of the European Communities v Kingdom of Sweden', 2005) …

Reference list

'Commission of the European Communities v Kingdom of Sweden' (2005) Case no. C-111/03. *European Court Reports,* I, 08789.

Example

In-text citation

The climate change resolution (United Nations General Assembly, 1994) …

Reference list

United Nations General Assembly (1994) *United Nations framework convention on climate change*. Resolution A/RES/48/189. Available at: http://daccess-dds-ny.un.org/doc/UNDOC/GEN/N94/036/43/PDF/N9403643.pdf?OpenElement (Accessed: 15 September 2015).

E14 International legal sources

E14.1 United Nations resolutions

For General Assembly resolutions place A/RES/ before the resolution number, for example A/RES/62/24.

For Security Council resolutions place S/RES/ before the resolution number, for example S/RES/1801.

Citation order:
- Organisation
- Year (in round brackets)
- Title (in italics)
- Resolution no.
- Available at: URL
- (Accessed: date)

E14.2 International treaties, conventions and accords

NB If possible, cite from the United Nations Treaty Series.

Citation order:
- Title of treaty (in italics)
- Year (in round brackets)
- Treaty number
- Publication title (in italics)
- Volume and page numbers

OR if viewed online:
- Available at: URL
- (Accessed: date)

E14.3 International Court of Justice (ICJ) cases

Documentation produced in hearing cases at the ICJ includes merits, written and oral proceedings, orders, judgements, press releases and correspondence.

Citation order:

- Case name (in single quotation marks)
- Year (in round brackets)
- *International Court of Justice cases*
- Publication type and date (if required)
- Available at: URL
- (Accessed: date)

E15 Government publications

Citation order:

- Name of government department
- Year of publication (in round brackets)
- Title (in italics)
- Place of publication: publisher
- Series (in brackets) – if applicable

OR if viewed online:

- Available at: URL
- (Accessed: date)

Many UK government publications may be accessed via https://www.gov.uk but you should use the specific author or department as the author, if given.

Examples

In-text citation

Prison numbers increased last year (Ministry of Justice, 2007) as did the disparity in medical care (Department of Health, 2004; 2008).

Reference list

Department of Health (2004) *Primary medical services allocations 2004/05*. Health Service Circular HSC 2004/003. Available at: http://www.dh.gov.uk/en/Publicationsandstatistics/Lettersandcirculars/Healthservicecirculars/DH_4071269 (Accessed: 21 June 2013).

Department of Health (2008) *Health inequalities: progress and next steps*. Available at: http://www.dh.gov.uk/en/Publicationsandstatistics/Publications/PublicationsPolicyAndGuidance/DH_085307 (Accessed: 18 June 2013).

Ministry of Justice (2007) *Sentencing statistics (annual)*. Available at: http://www.justice.gov.uk/publications/sentencingannual.htm (Accessed: 3 June 2013).

NB If you are referencing government publications from more than one country, include the country of origin (in round brackets) after the department name.

Examples

In-text citation

The UK and Canada oppose the use of landmines (Department for International Development (UK), 2010; Department of Foreign Affairs and International Trade (Canada), 2012).

Reference list

Department for International Development (UK) (2010) *Creating a safer environment: clearing landmines and other explosive remnants of war*. Available at: https://www.gov.uk/government/publications/demining-strategy-2010-2013 (Accessed: 5 January 2013).

Department of Foreign Affairs and International Trade (Canada) (2012) *Reaffirming the commitment*. Available at: http://www.international.gc.ca/mines/documents/cnd-fund-fond-can/00-01-introduction.aspx?lang=eng&view=d (Accessed: 5 January 2013).

E16   Publications of international organisations

Citation order:
- Name of organisation or institution
- Year of publication (in round brackets)
- Title (in italics)
- Place of publication: publisher

OR if viewed online:
- Available at: URL
- (Accessed: date)

Examples

In-text citation

Reports by the European Commission (2013), the United Nations (2011) and International Chamber of Commerce, Commission for Air Transport (2015) …

Reference list

European Commission (2013) *Making globalisation work for everyone*. Luxembourg: Office for Official Publications of the European Communities.

International Chamber of Commerce, Commission for Air Transport (2015) *The need for greater liberalization in international air transport*. Available at: http://www.iccwbo.org/Advocacy-Codes-and-Rules/Document-centre/2015/The-need-forgreater-liberalization-of-international-airtransport/ (Accessed: 9 February 2016).

United Nations (2011) *Yearbook of the United Nations, 2007 vol. 61*. New York: United Nations Department of Public Information.

E17 Scientific and technical information

E17.1 Technical standards

Citation order:

- Name of authorising organisation
- Year of publication (in round brackets)
- Number and title of standard (in italics)
- Place of publication: publisher

OR if viewed online:

- Available at: URL
- (Accessed: date)

Examples

In-text citation

Loft conversions are subject to strict controls (British Standards Institution, 2004).

Reference list

British Standards Institution (2004) *BSEN1995-1-2:2004: Design of timber structures*. London: British Standards Institution.

OR
British Standards Institution (2004) *BSEN1995-1-2:2004: Design of timber structures*. Available at: http://www.standardsuk.com/products/BS-EN-1995-1-2-2004.php (Accessed: 30 June 2015).

E17.2 Patents

Citation order:

- Inventor(s)
- Year of publication (in round brackets)
- Title (in italics)
- Authorising organisation
- Patent number
- Available at: URL
- (Accessed: date)

Example

In-text citation

Padley (2012) proposed a solution.

Reference list

Padley, S. (2012) *Radiator isolating valve*. UK Intellectual Property Office Patent no. GB2463069. Available at: http://www.ipo.gov.uk/p-find-publication (Accessed: 24 August 2015).

E17.3 Scientific datasets

Reference where you located the data, for example journal article/book/online.

Citation order:
- Author
- Date (in round brackets)
- Title of data (in single quotation marks)
- Available at: URL
- (Accessed: date)

> **Example**
>
> **In-text citation**
>
> The data (Ralchenko *et al.*, 2014) proved …
>
> **Reference list**
>
> Ralchenko, Y. *et al.* (2014) 'Na levels holdings'. Available at: http://physics.nist.gov/asd3 (Accessed: 2 August 2015).
>
> OR, if your **institution requires referencing of all named authors**:
>
> Ralchenko, Y., Kramida, A.E., Reader, J., and NIST ASD Team (2014) 'Na levels holdings'. Available at: http://physics.nist.gov/asd3 (Accessed: 2 August 2015).

E17.4 Requests for Comments (RFCs)

Citation order:
- Author/editor
- Year (in round brackets)
- Title (in italics)
- Document number
- Available at: URL
- (Accessed: date)

> **Example**
>
> **In-text citation**
>
> A number of comments were made relating to the document (Hoffman and Harris, 2015).
>
> **Reference list**
>
> Hoffman, P. and Harris, S. (2015) *The Tao of IETF: a novice's guide to the Internet Engineering Task Force.* Nos: FYI 17 and RFC 4677. Available at: http://tools.ietf.org/html/rfc4677 (Accessed: 20 October 2015).

E17.5 Mathematical equations

Reference where you located the equation, for example online journal article.

Citation order:
- Author
- Year of publication (in round brackets)
- Title of article (in single quotation marks)
- Title of journal (in italics – capitalise first letter of each word in title, except for linking words such as and, of, the, for)
- Volume, issue, page numbers
- Available at: URL (or doi if available)
- (Accessed: date) (not required when doi used)

> **Example**
>
> **In-text citation**
>
> Fradelizi and Meyer (2008, p. 1449) noted that for $z > 0$
>
> $$P(K) \geq \frac{e^{n+1-z} z^{n+1}}{(n!)^2}$$
>
> …
>
> **Reference list**
>
> Fradelizi, M. and Meyer, M. (2008) 'Some functional inverse Santaló inequalities', *Advances in Mathematics*, 218(5), pp. 1430–1452. doi: 10.1016/j.aim.2008.03.013.

E17.6 Graphs

Reference where you located the graph, for example graph in a book (give book details).

Citation order:

- Author
- Year of publication (in round brackets)
- Title of book (in italics)
- Place of publication: publisher
- Page number or figure number for graph
- Graph

Example

In-text citation

The effects of the compounds (Day and Gastel, 2006, p. 95) …

Reference list

Day, R. and Gastel, B. (2006) *How to write and publish a scientific paper.* Cambridge: Cambridge University Press, p. 95, graph.

E18 Reviews

Citation order:

- Name of the reviewer (if indicated)
- Year of publication of the review (in round brackets)
- Title of the review (in single quotation marks)
- Review of … (title of work reviewed – in italics)
- Author/director of work being reviewed
- Publication details (title in italics)

OR if viewed online:

- Available at: URL
- (Accessed: date)

E18.1 Book reviews

Example

In-text citation

Darden (2007) considered the book …

Reference list

Darden, L. (2007) 'Cell division'. Review of *Discovering cell mechanisms: the creation of modern cell biology*, by William Bechtel. *Journal of the History of Biology,* 40(1), pp. 185–187.

E18.2 Drama reviews

Example

In-text citation

One reviewer (Billington, 2008, p. 19) wrote …

Reference list

Billington, M. (2008) 'The main event'. Review of *On the rocks*, by D.H. Lawrence. Hampstead Theatre, London. *The Guardian* (Review section), 5 July, p. 19.

E18.3   Film reviews

Examples

`In-text citation`

Barnes (1989) and Parsons (2010) thought it a classic film.

`Reference list`

Magazine review
Barnes, L. (1989) 'Citizen Kane'. Review of *Citizen Kane*, directed by Orson Welles (RKO). *New Vision*, 9 October, pp. 24–25.

Internet review
Parsons, T. (2010) 'A rosebud by any other name'. Review of *Citizen Kane*, directed by Orson Welles. Available at: http://www.imdb.com/title/tt0033467/reviews?start=210 (Accessed: 5 July 2015).

E18.4   Reviews of musical performances

Example

`In-text citation`

Hickling (2008) thought it 'a little touch of magic'.

`Reference list`

Hickling, A. (2008) 'The opera'. Review of *Don Giovanni*, by Mozart. New Vic, Newcastle-under-Lyme. *The Guardian* (Review section), 5 July, p. 19.

E19   Visual sources

The internet has revolutionised the availability of visual sources such as images, maps and artistic works. Some examples will show how to cite and reference the original works and online versions.

E19.1   Exhibitions

Citation order:

- Title of exhibition (in italics)
- Year (in round brackets)
- [Exhibition]
- Location. Date(s) of exhibition

Example

`In-text citation`

The acclaimed exhibition in London is one of the finest (*Pre-Raphaelites: Victorian Avant-Garde*, 2012).

`Reference list`

Pre-Raphaelites: Victorian Avant-Garde (2012) [Exhibition]. Tate Britain, London. 12 September 2012–13 January 2013.

E19.2   Paintings/drawings

Citation order:

- Artist
- Year (if available)
- Title of the work (in italics)
- Medium (in square brackets)
- Institution or collection that houses the work, followed by the city

OR if seen online:

- Available at: URL
- (Accessed: date)

Examples

`In-text citation`

Works by Coello (1664) and Dalí (1958) …

`Reference list`

Coello, C. (1664) *The triumph of St Augustine* [Oil on canvas]. Museo del Prado, Madrid.

Dalí, S. (1958) *Madonna* [Oil on canvas]. Available at: http://www.oxfordartonline.com (Accessed: 9 July 2015).

E19.3 Sculpture, statues and memorials

E19.3 a. Sculpture

Citation order:

- Sculptor
- Year (in round brackets)
- Title (in italics)
- [Sculpture]
- Gallery or name of collection

OR if viewed online, add:

- Available at: URL
- (Accessed: date)

> **Example**
>
> **In-text citation**
>
> His talents were proven with *The lovers* (Rodin, 1886).
>
> **Reference list**
>
> Rodin, A. (1886) *The lovers* [Sculpture]. Private collection.

E19.3 b. Statues

Citation order:

- Sculptor
- Year (in round brackets)
- Title (in italics)
- [Statue]
- Location (and/or GPS coordinates, if available)
- (Viewed: date)

> **Example**
>
> **In-text citation**
>
> The admiral's statue (Melton, 2000) looks across the Channel to France.
>
> **Reference list**
>
> Melton, S. (2000) *Admiral Sir Bertram Home Ramsey* [Statue]. Dover Castle, Kent, England, GPS coordinates: 51° 7' 36.29" N, 1° 19' 26.22" E. (Viewed: 8 August 2012).

E19.3 c. Memorials

Citation order:

- Name of architect (if known); if not, use name of memorial
- Date of construction (in round brackets)
- Name of memorial (in italics)
- Location (and/or GPS coordinates, if available)
- (Viewed: date)

> **Example**
>
> **In-text citation**
>
> The memorial (Leong Swee Lim, 1967) …
>
> **Reference list**
>
> Leong Swee Lim (1967) *Civilian War Memorial*, War Memorial Park, Beach Road, Singapore, GPS coordinates: 1°17' 32.91" N, 103° 51' 11.11" E. (Viewed: 4 February 2012).

E19.4 Inscriptions

E19.4 a. Inscriptions on monuments

Inscriptions on gravestones and memorials are, in many instances, the only detailed record of a person's existence, circumstances and relationships, apart from basic information given in birth, marriage and death certificates and the census.

Referencing this source can be difficult, but (as with printed material) you should aim to provide as much information as possible for another person to locate the gravestone or memorial. In some instances, the plot number of a grave will be obtainable and can be referenced; if not, try to give an indication of the location from a landmark.

Citation order:
- Name of deceased (in single quotation marks)
- Year of death/event (in round brackets)
- [Monument inscription]
- Location
- (Viewed: date)

Examples

In-text citation

The gravestone of the railway engineman ('Oswald Gardiner', 1840) compares him to one of the locomotives he drove: 'My engine now is cold and still. No water does my boilor fill.'

Reference list

'Oswald Gardiner' (1840) [Monument inscription] St Mary the Virgin Churchyard (5m northwest of church), Whickham, Tyne and Wear (Viewed: 12 August 2012).

In-text citation

Corporal Pears was killed during the retreat to Dunkirk ('Wilfrid Pears', 1940).

Reference list

Where plot number available
'Wilfred Pears' (1940) [Monument inscription] Plot 13, row E, grave 13, London Cemetery and Extension, Longueval, France (Viewed: 27 July 2014).

E19.4   b. Inscriptions on statues

Referencing inscriptions on statues can also be difficult, as the author may not be identified and the wording may be a quotation from an earlier source. Give as much information as you are able to.

Citation order:
- Author (if known); if not, use title of statue (in italics)
- Year of inscription (in round brackets)
- Inscription on statue to/of … (in italics)
- Location
- (Viewed: date)

Example

In-text citation

The inscription by Herbert (2000) …

Reference list

Herbert, A.P. (2000) *Inscription on statue to Admiral Bertram Home Ramsey*, Dover Castle, Kent, England (Viewed: 8 August 2012).

E19.4   c. Inscriptions on buildings

Citation order:
- Author (if known); if not, use first three words of inscription
- Year of inscription (in round brackets)
- Inscription on … (in italics)
- Location
- (Viewed: date)

Example

In-text citation

The exterior inscription by Lewis (2004) …

Reference list

Lewis, G. (2004) *Inscription on Wales Millennium Centre*, Cardiff Bay, Cardiff, Wales (Viewed: 8 August 2012).

E19.5 Displays

E19.5 a. Installations/exhibits

Citation order:

- Artist
- Year (in round brackets)
- Title of installation or exhibit (in italics)
- [Installation] or [Exhibit]
- Gallery or location
- (Viewed: date)

> **Example**
>
> **In-text citation**
>
> *My bed* by Tracey Emin (1999) …
>
> **Reference list**
>
> Emin, T. (1999) *My bed* [Installation]. Tate Gallery, London (Viewed: 31 October 2000).

E19.5 b. Graffiti

By its nature, graffiti is anonymous (even when the graffitist includes their signature tag). It is usually short-lived artistic expression (or vandalism, depending on one's perspective). As it may be removed at any time, it is essential to include as much information as possible to describe the content, location and date viewed. Be careful if citing offensive language or imagery in graffiti.

Citation order:

- Title or description (with graffitist's tag, if present) (in italics)
- Year (in round brackets)
- [Graffiti]
- Location
- (Viewed: date)

> **Example**
>
> **In-text citation**
>
> The graffiti (*Marty u dare!*, 2012) demonstrated …
>
> **Reference list**
>
> *Marty u dare!* (2012) [Graffiti] 3 Westland Street, Londonderry, Northern Ireland. (Viewed: 27 June 2012).

E19.6 Photographs/images

Students often become confused when referencing works of art they have photographed. They are unsure whether to reference themselves as the image maker or to reference the work itself. The answer is clear: you reference what you are referring to (that is, your photograph or the work of art). Thus, if you wish to discuss the way you photographed a sculpture by Rodin, you would reference yourself, following the examples below (omitting, if necessary, place of publication and publisher). If, however, you photographed Rodin's sculpture in a gallery and you are discussing the sculpture itself, you would follow the guidelines in Sections E19.3 or E19.5.

NB For images that you download onto edevices, and to which you still have access, you should replace accessed date with downloaded date.

E19.6 a. Prints or slides

Citation order:

- Photographer
- Year (in round brackets)
- Title of photograph (in italics)
- [Photograph]
- Place of publication: publisher (if available)

Example

In-text citation

The seasonal and architectural changes were captured on film (Thomas, 2013).

Reference list

Thomas, T. (2013) *Redevelopment in Byker* [Photograph]. Newcastle upon Tyne: Then & Now Publishing.

E19.6   b. Photographs from the internet

Citation order:

- Photographer
- Year of publication (in round brackets)
- Title of photograph (in italics)
- Available at: URL
- (Accessed/downloaded: date)

Example

In-text citation

His beautiful photograph (Kitto, 2013) ...

Reference list

Kitto, J. (2013) *Golden sunset.* Available at: http://www.jameskitto.co.uk/photo_1827786.html (Accessed: 14 June 2015).

E19.6   c. Photographs in online collections

On occasions, you may need to reference images that you have found through social media sites such as *Pinterest* or *Tumblr*, or that you have viewed directly on *Flickr*. You may also use sites like *Instagram* to view photographs or videos or upload your own. Do not be confused: you simply take the reader to where you viewed or uploaded the image or video.

Citation order:

- Photographer

- Year of publication (in round brackets)
- Title of photograph/video (or collection) (in italics)
- Available at: URL
- (Accessed/downloaded: date)

Example: *Tumblr*

In-text citation

Solar ikon's recent work (2014) ...

Reference list

Solar ikon (2014) *Green onion*. Available at: http://www.tumblr.com/tagged/food (Accessed: 13 June 2015).

Example: *Flickr*

In-text citation

Chunyang Lin's (Solar ikon) recent work (2015) ...

Reference list

Lin, C. (2015) *Green onion*. Available at: http://www.flickr.com/photos/chunyang/4004866489/ (Downloaded: 13 June 2015).

Example: *Instagram*

In-text citation

Fisher's collection of deconstruction photographs (2016) ...

Reference list

Fisher, D. (2016) *deepbody*. Available at: https://instagram.com/deepbody/ (Accessed: 25 April 2016).

E19.6   d. Clip art

If using clip art images from online collections, use the details you are given to take the reader to the relevant piece of artwork. Be aware that some of the citation order details may not always be available.

Citation order:
- Producer
- Year of publication (in round brackets)
- Title of clip art (in italics)
- Available at: URL
- (Accessed/downloaded: date)

> **Example:**
>
> **In-text citation**
>
> The image of the dog (*Dogs*, 2015) …
>
> **Reference list**
>
> *Dogs* (2015) Available at: http://www.clipart.co.uk/cgi-bin/icdisplay.pl?1,dog,1 (Accessed: 15 October 2015).

E19.6 e. Medical images

Many kinds of medical/anatomical images can be viewed and downloaded from the internet (for example MRI, PET, CT and ultrasound scans, and X-rays) for use in supporting your arguments or demonstrating particular aspects of anatomical or medical information. These would simply be referenced as photographs/images from the internet (see Section E19.6b).

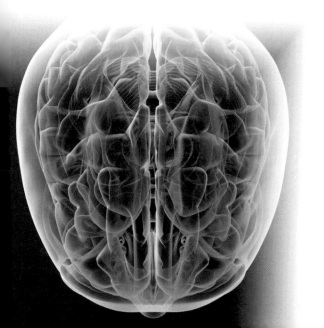

Other images may be found in online databases such as *Anatomy TV*. For these, use the following format.

Citation order:
- Image title (in italics)
- Year (in round brackets)
- Medium (in square brackets)
- Available at: URL
- (Accessed/downloaded: date)

> **Example**
>
> **In-text citation**
>
> The X-ray and scan (*The spine*, 2013) clearly showed …
>
> **Reference list**
>
> *The spine* (2013) [X-ray and MRI scan]. Available at: http://www.anatomy.tv/new_home.aspx (Accessed: 28 July 2015).

However, if you are working on placement in a hospital, there will be occasions when you may want to reference an individual patient's scan, for example. These are confidential sources of information, and as such these images would need to be anonymised (as shown in Section E4.5), and the patient's and hospital's permission obtained if you wanted to use the image in your text/appendices. In these circumstances, use the following format.

Citation order:
- Anonymised patient's name (in square brackets)
- Year image produced (in round brackets)
- Image title (in italics)
- Medium (in square brackets)
- Location
- Institution

E19.7   Packaging

Citation order:

- Manufacturer
- Year seen (in round brackets)
- Product name (in italics)
- Medium (in square brackets)

OR if seen online, add:

- Available at: URL
- (Accessed: date)

Examples

In-text citation

The different forms of packaging (The Premier Foods Group, 2012; Mars Incorporated, 2013) …

Reference list

Mars Incorporated (2013) *Mars Bar* [Wrapper].

The Premier Foods Group (2012) *Loyd Grossman tomato and mushroom sauce* [Jar label]. Available at: www. loydgrossmansauces.co.uk (Accessed: 23 May 2015).

E19.8   Book illustrations, figures, diagrams, logos and tables

Citation order:

- Author of book
- Year of publication (in round brackets)
- Title of book (in italics)

- Place of publication: publisher
- Page reference of illustration and so on
- illus./fig./diagram/logo/table

Example

In-text citation

Holbein's painting illustrated the prelate's ornate mitre (Strong, 1990, pp. 62–63).

Reference list

Strong, R. (1990) *Lost treasures of Britain*. London: Viking, pp. 62–63, illus.

OR if seen online, reference as shown in Sections E8.1–2 and add Medium (in square brackets).

Example

In-text citation

Controversy surrounded the Olympic logo (London2012, 2010) …

Reference list

London2012 (2010) *London2012* [Logo]. Available at: http://www.london2012.com (Accessed: 23 May 2015).

E19.9   Cartoons

Citation order:

- Artist
- Date (if available)
- Title of cartoon (in single quotation marks)
- [Cartoon]
- Title of publication (in italics)
- Day and month

OR if seen online add:

- Available at: URL
- (Accessed: date)

Example

In-text citation

Steve Bell (2008) warned of the danger …

Reference list

Bell, S. (2008) 'Don't let this happen' [Cartoon]. *The Guardian*, 19 June. Available at: http://www.guardian.co.uk/world/cartoon/2008/jun/19/steve.bell.afghanistan.troops (Accessed: 2 July 2015).

E19.10 Comics

Comic books and graphic novels are referenced as books (see Section E1).

To reference an *entire issue of a comic*, use the following:

Citation order:

- Author (if available)
- Title of comic (in italics)
- Year of publication (in round brackets)
- Day, month, issue number (use the elements that are given)

Example

In-text citation

The latest issue (*Commando*, 2015) …

Reference list

Commando (2015) 12 September, no. 4814.

To reference a *comic strip*, use the following:

Citation order:

- Author (if available)
- Title of comic strip (in single quotation marks)
- Year of publication (in round brackets)
- Title of comic (in italics)
- Day, month, issue number, page (use the elements that are given)

Example

In-text citation

Jessica Ennis starred as Ennis the Menace in the hilarious comic strip ('The menace heptathlon', 2012).

Reference list

'The menace heptathlon' (2012) *The Beano*, 25 August, pp. 30–31.

E19.11 Posters

Citation order:

- Artist (if known, or use title)
- Year (in round brackets)
- Title (in italics)
- [Poster]
- Exhibited at
- Location and date(s) of exhibition
- Dimensions (if relevant and available)

Example: poster copy of painting

In-text citation

The image (Chagall, no date) …

Reference list

Chagall, M. (no date) *Le violiniste* [Poster]. 84cm x 48cm/33" x 19".

Example: poster for exhibition

In-text citation

Smith's poster (2003) …

Reference list

Smith, K. (2003) *Prints, books and things* [Poster]. Exhibited at New York, Museum of Modern Art. 5 December 2003 to 8 March 2004.

E19.12 Mood boards

Citation order:

- Designer (if known)
- Year (in round brackets)
- Title (in italics)
- [Mood board]
- Presented at
- Location and date(s) of presentation

OR if presented online:

- Available at: URL
- (Accessed: date)

Example

In-text citation

His highly effective mood board (Weitzel, 2011) …

Reference list

Weitzel, L. (2011) *Say cheese.* [Mood board]. Available at: http://flickr.com/photos/daisies7/5857970176/ (Accessed: 12 June 2015).

E19.13 Postcards

Citation order:

- Artist (if available)
- Year (in round brackets if available)
- Title (in italics)
- [Postcard]
- Place of publication: publisher

Example

In-text citation

The flat sandy beach (Corrance, no date) …

Reference list

Corrance, D. (no date) *Gairloch, Wester Ross* [Postcard]. Scotland: Stirling Gallery.

E19.14 Maps

E19.14 a. Ordnance Survey maps

Citation order:

- Ordnance Survey
- Year of publication (in round brackets)
- Title (in italics)
- Sheet number, scale
- Place of publication: publisher
- Series (in round brackets)

Example

`In-text citation`

Archaeological sites are italicised (Ordnance Survey, 2002).

`Reference list`

Ordnance Survey (2002) *Preston and Blackpool*, sheet 102, 1:50,000. Southampton: Ordnance Survey (Landranger series).

E19.14 b. Geological Survey maps

Citation order:

- Corporate author and publisher
- Year of publication (in round brackets)
- Title (in italics)
- Sheet number, scale
- Place of publication: publisher
- Series (in round brackets)

Example

`In-text citation`

The landscape has undergone profound changes since the map (Ordnance Survey, 1980) was printed.

`Reference list`

Ordnance Survey (1980) *Bellingham (solid)*, sheet 13, 1:50,000. Southampton: Ordnance Survey. (Geological Survey of Great Britain [England and Wales]).

E19.14 c. Online maps

Citation order:

- Map publisher
- Year of publication (in round brackets)
- Title of map section (in single quotation marks)
- Sheet number or tile, scale
- Available at: URL
- (Accessed: date)

Examples

Ordnance Survey

`In-text citation`

The leisure centre is close to Tiddenfoot Lake (Ordnance Survey, 2013).

`Reference list`

Ordnance Survey (2013) 'Tiddenfoot Lake', Tile sp92sw, 1:10,000. Available at: http://edina.ac.uk/digimap/ (Accessed: 3 May 2015).

Google Maps

`In-text citation`

The dock layout and road network can be seen using *Google Maps* (Tele Atlas, 2015).

`Reference list`

Tele Atlas (2015) 'Cardiff Bay'. Available at: http://maps.google.co.uk (Accessed: 5 July 2015).

E20 Live performances

E20.1 Concerts

Citation order:

- Composer
- Year of performance (in round brackets)
- Title (in italics)
- Performed by … conducted by …
- [Location. Date seen]

Examples

Classical concert

> **In-text citation**
>
> A wonderful premiere (Lord, 2007) …

> **Reference list**
>
> Lord, J. (2007) *Durham Concerto.* Performed by the Liverpool Philharmonic Orchestra conducted by Mischa Damev [Durham Cathedral, Durham. 20 October].

Band concert

> **In-text citation**
>
> The Kings of Leon (2008) wowed the crowd …

> **Reference list**
>
> Kings of Leon (2008) [Glastonbury Festival. 27 June].

E20.2 Dance

Citation order:

- Composer or choreographer
- Year of premiere (in round brackets)
- Title (in italics)
- [Location. Date seen]

Example

> **In-text citation**
>
> The performance was true to the intentions of its creator (Ashton, 1937).

> **Reference list**
>
> Ashton, F. (1937) *A wedding bouquet* [Royal Opera House, London. 22 October 2004].

E20.3 Plays

Citation order:

- Title (in italics)
- by Author
- Year of performance (in round brackets)
- Directed by
- [Location. Date seen]

Example

> **In-text citation**
>
> One innovation was the use of Sellotape for the fairies' webs (*A midsummer night's dream,* 1995).

> **Reference list**
>
> *A midsummer night's dream* by William Shakespeare (1995) Directed by Ian Judge [Theatre Royal, Newcastle upon Tyne. 26 February].

E21 Audiovisual material

The internet has radically altered access to audio and visual sources and created the means for anyone to produce and distribute material. You may also view or hear programmes through catch-up services such as *BBC iPlayer*, *ITV Hub*, *All 4*, *Demand 5* and *Sky Go* on a variety of devices. You do not need to specify the catch-up service or the device. The nature of the material and the facts necessary to identify or retrieve it should dictate the substance of your in-text citations and reference list. The examples cite and reference traditional and online access routes.

E21.1 Radio

E21.1 a. Radio programmes

Citation order:
- Title of programme (in italics)
- Year of transmission (in round brackets)
- Name of channel
- Date of transmission (day/month)

Example

`In-text citation`

The latest report (*Today*, 2016) …

`Reference list`

Today (2016) BBC Radio 4, 15 April.

E21.1 b. Radio programmes heard on the internet

You may listen to radio programmes live on the internet, or days after the original transmission through services such as the BBC's *iPlayer*. Specify the full date of the original broadcast as well as the date you accessed the programme.

Citation order:
- Title of programme (in italics)
- Year of original transmission (in round brackets)
- Name of channel
- Day and month of original transmission
- Available at: URL
- (Accessed: date)

Example

`In-text citation`

Technology offers the means to improve human ability (*Redesigning the human body*, 2013) …

`Reference list`

Redesigning the human body (2013) BBC Radio 4, 25 September. Available at: http://www.bbc.co.uk/radio4/redesigninghumanbody/ (Accessed: 15 June 2015).

E21.2 Television

E21.2 a. Television programmes

Citation order:
- Title of programme (in italics)
- Year of broadcast (in round brackets)
- Name of channel
- Broadcast date (day/month)

Example

`In-text citation`

The embarrassing corporate wannabes (*The Apprentice*, 2015) …

`Reference list`

The Apprentice (2015) BBC One Television, 23 September.

To quote something a character/presenter has said:

Example

`In-text citation`

'You're fired!' (Sugar, 2012) …

`Reference list`

Sugar, A. (2012) *The Apprentice*. BBC One Television, 23 June.

E21.2 b. Episodes of a television series

Citation order:

- Title of episode (in single quotation marks)
- Year of broadcast (in round brackets)
- Title of programme (in italics)
- Series and episode numbers
- Name of channel
- Broadcast date (day/month)

Example

In-text citation

Some Daleks were mad and bad ('Asylum of the Daleks', 2012).

Reference list

'Asylum of the Daleks' (2012) *Doctor Who*, Series 33, episode 1. BBC One Television, 1 September.

E21.2 c. Television programmes/ series on DVD/Blu-ray

Citation order:

- Title of episode (in single quotation marks)
- Year of distribution (in round brackets)
- Title of programme/series (in italics)
- Series and episode numbers (if known)
- Director and writer
- Date of original broadcast (if known)
- [DVD] or [Blu-ray]
- Place of distribution: distribution company

Example

In-text citation

The origins of the Doctor's most fearsome foe were revealed in 'Genesis of the Daleks' (2006).

Reference list

'Genesis of the Daleks' (2006) *Doctor Who,* episode 1. Directed by David Maloney. Written by Terry Nation. First broadcast 1975 [DVD]. London: BBC DVD.

E21.2 d. Separate episodes from DVD/Blu-ray box-sets

Citation order:

- Title of episode (in single quotation marks)
- Year of distribution (in round brackets)
- Title of programme/series (in italics)
- 'In'
- Title of compilation or box-set (in italics)
- [DVD] or [Blu-ray]
- Place of distribution: distribution company

Example

In-text citation

Close attention was paid to period details ('Episode 8', 2014) …

Reference list

'Episode 8' (2014) *Downton Abbey* In *Downton Abbey Series 5* [DVD] London: Universal Pictures UK.

E21.2 e. Television programmes viewed on the internet

Citation order:

- Title of episode (in single quotation marks) if known; if not, use title of programme
- Year of broadcast (in round brackets)
- Title of programme/series (in italics)

- Series and episode numbers (if known)
- Name of channel
- Broadcast date (day/month)
- Available at: URL
- (Accessed: date)

Example

`In-text citation`

The restoration of the lifeboat station was broadcast on *Grand Designs* ('Tenby', 2011).

`Reference list`

'Tenby' (2011) *Grand Designs*, Series 7, episode 30, Channel 4 Television, 28 September. Available at: http://www. channel4.com/programmes/granddesigns/ episode-guide/series-7/ episode-30 (Accessed: 15 January 2016).

E21.3   Audio/video downloads

NB For audiobooks, see Section E1.4.

Music downloads are available from a range of different websites including *iTunes*, *Amazon Music*, *Spotify* and the band's or artist's website. When you have downloaded music onto an edevice, you may find it helpful to add a general statement at the end of your reference list informing your tutor that the track(s) is(are) available on your edevice.

Citation order:

- Author/singer/artist (if available; if not use title first)
- Year of distribution (in round brackets)
- Title of recording/video (in italics)
- Available at: URL
- (Downloaded: date)

Example

`In-text citation`

Their highly acclaimed album (The Civil Wars, 2012) …

`Reference list`

The Civil Wars (2012) *Barton Hollow*. Available at: http://www.myplaydirect. com/the-civil-wars (Downloaded: 5 August 2015).

E21.4   Music or spoken word recordings on audio CDs or vinyl

E21.4   a. Tracks released on CD or vinyl as singles

Citation order:

- Artist
- Year of distribution (in round brackets)
- Title of track (in italics)
- [CD] or [vinyl]
- Place of distribution: distribution company

Example

`In-text citation`

Her recent release (Jessie J, 2012) …

`Reference list`

Jessie J (2012) *Domino* [CD]. New York, NY: Universal Republic Records.

E21.4   b. Tracks on a CD or vinyl album

Citation order:

- Artist
- Year of distribution (in round brackets)
- Title of track (in single quotation marks)
- Title of album (in italics)
- [CD] or [vinyl]
- Place of distribution: distribution company

E21.4   c. Whole albums

Citation order:

- Artist
- Year of distribution (in round brackets)
- Title of album (in italics)
- [CD] or [vinyl]
- Place of distribution: distribution company

Example

In-text citation

The band's acclaimed album (Emily Barker & The Red Clay Halo, 2008) …

Reference list

Emily Barker & The Red Clay Halo (2008) *Despite the snow* [CD]. London: Everyone Sang.

E21.5   Music or spoken word recordings on audio cassettes

Citation order:

- Artist (if available; if not use title in italics first)
- Year of distribution (in round brackets)
- Title of recording (in italics)
- [Audio cassette]
- Place of publication: publisher

Example

In-text citation

Determination is a key attribute (*It's your choice: selection skills for managers*, 1993).

Reference list

It's your choice: selection skills for managers (1993) [Audio cassette]. London: Video Arts.

E21.6   Liner notes

The liner notes in CD, DVD, vinyl and cassette containers often have information that can be referenced.

Citation order:

- Author
- Year (in round brackets)
- Title of liner notes text (in single quotation marks)
- 'in'
- Title of recording (in italics)
- [CD liner notes]
- Place of distribution: distribution company

Example

In-text citation

Thrills (1997, p. 11) described Weller's lyrics as 'sheer poetry'.

Reference list

Thrills, A. (1997) 'What a catalyst he turned out to be', in *The very best of The Jam* [CD liner notes]. London: Polydor.

E21.7   Lyrics from songs/hymns

Citation order:

- Lyricist
- Year of distribution (in round brackets)
- Title of song/hymn (in italics)
- Place of distribution: distribution company

> **Example**
>
> **In-text citation**
>
> Lennon and McCartney (1966) expressed the frustration of every new author: 'Dear Sir or Madam, will you read my book? It took me years to write, will you take a look?'
>
> **Reference list**
>
> Lennon, J. and McCartney, P. (1966) *Paperback writer*. Liverpool: Northern Songs Ltd.

E21.8 Musical scores (sheet music)

Citation order:

- Composer
- Year of publication (in round brackets)
- Title of score (in italics)
- Notes
- Place of publication: publisher

> **Example**
>
> **In-text citation**
>
> The composer's evocation of the sea in *The Hebrides* (Mendelssohn, 1999) …
>
> **Reference list**
>
> Mendelssohn, F. (1999) *The Hebrides*. Edited from composer's notes by John Wilson. London: Initial Music Publishing.

E21.9 Films/movies

E21.9 a. Films/movies in film format

Citation order:

- Title of film (in italics)
- Year of distribution (in round brackets)
- Directed by
- [Film]
- Place of distribution: distribution company

> **Example**
>
> **In-text citation**
>
> Movies were used to attack President Bush's policies (*Fahrenheit 9/11*, 2004).
>
> **Reference list**
>
> *Fahrenheit 9/11* (2004) Directed by Michael Moore [Film]. Santa Monica, Calif.: Lions Gate Films.

E21.9 b. Films on DVD/Blu-ray

Citation order:

- Title of film (in italics)
- Year of distribution (in round brackets)
- Directed by
- [DVD] or [Blu-ray]
- Place of distribution: distribution company

> **Example**
>
> **In-text citation**
>
> Special effects can dominate a film, for example *The Matrix reloaded* (2003).
>
> **Reference list**
>
> *The Matrix reloaded* (2003) Directed by A. & L. Wachowski [DVD]. Los Angeles, Calif.: Warner Bros Inc.

For *films that have been reissued* use the following format:

Citation order:

- Title of film (in italics)
- Year of original film distribution (in round brackets)
- Directed by
- [DVD] or [Blu-ray]
- Reissued
- Place of distribution: distributor company
- Year of reissue

Example

In-text citation

… in this breathtaking, poetic film (*Pink narcissus,* 1971).

Reference list

Pink narcissus (1971) Directed by J. Bidgood [DVD]. Reissued, London: BFI, 2007.

Thus, just the year of the original film distribution is given in-text. The reference list also includes the date of reissue.

Many films on DVD/Blu-ray come with additional material on other disks, such as interviews with actors and directors and outtakes. Sections E21.9c–d give examples for referencing some of this material.

E21.9   c. Directors' commentaries on DVD/Blu-ray

Citation order:

- Name of commentator
- Year (in round brackets)
- Director's commentary (in single quotation marks)
- Name of film (in italics)
- Directed by
- [DVD] or [Blu-ray]
- Place of distribution: distribution company

Example

In-text citation

The director thought this was a profitable franchise (Wachowski, 2003).

Reference list

Wachowski, A. (2003) 'Director's commentary', *The Matrix reloaded.* Directed by A. & L. Wachowski [DVD]. Los Angeles, Calif.: Warner Bros Inc.

E21.9   d. Interviews with film directors

Citation order:

- Name of person interviewed
- Year of interview (in round brackets)
- Title of the interview (if any) (in single quotation marks)
- Interview with/interviewed by
- Interviewer's name
- Title of film (in italics)
- [DVD] or [Blu-ray]
- Place of distribution: distribution company

Example

In-text citation

The director thought this was a profitable franchise (Wachowski, 2003).

Reference list

Wachowski, A. (2003) 'Interview with A. Wachowski'. Interviewed by L. Jones. *The Matrix reloaded* [DVD]. Los Angeles, Calif.: Warner Bros Inc.

E21.9   e. Films on video cassettes

Citation order:

- Title of film or programme (in italics)
- Year of distribution (in round brackets)
- Directed by
- [Video cassette]
- Place of distribution: distribution company

E21.9 f. Films on *YouTube*

Citation order:

- Name of person posting video
- Year video posted (in round brackets)
- Title of film or programme (in italics)
- Available at: URL
- (Accessed: date)

E21.10 Podcasts

Although podcasts can be downloaded onto portable devices, you should reference where it was published or displayed for download rather than trying to give your edevice as a source.

Citation order:

- Author/presenter
- Year that the site was published/last updated (in round brackets)
- Title of podcast (in italics)
- [Podcast]

- Day/month of posted message
- Available at: URL
- (Accessed: date)

E21.11 Phonecasts

Phonecasts are audio or video programmes transmitted to a user's mobile phone. The user dials a number to access the programme. Alternatively, phonecasters can broadcast by using their telephones in place of microphones. Although phone calls are personal communications, it is possible to reference phonecasts if the access details are available in a publication or web page.

Citation order:

- Title of phonecast (in italics)
- Year of production (in round brackets)
- [Phonecast]
- Available at: URL
- (Accessed: date)

Example

In-text citation

Zuckerberg created *Facebook* in 2004 (*A conversation with Mark Zuckerberg*, 2007).

Reference list

A conversation with Mark Zuckerberg (2007) [Phonecast]. Available at: http://www.phonecasting.com/Channel/ViewChannel.aspx?Id=1904 (Accessed: 11 July 2015).

E21.12 Screencasts

Also called 'video screen captures', screencasts are digital recordings of computer screen activity. Screencast videos can provide instructions for using software applications.

Citation order:

- Title of screencast (in italics)
- Year of production (in round brackets)
- [Screencast]
- Available at: URL
- (Accessed: date)

Example

In-text citation

An online video demonstrated functions (*Learning Rails the zombie way*, no date).

Reference list

Learning Rails the zombie way (no date) [Screencast]. Available at: http://www.rubyonrails.org/screencasts (Accessed: 27 January 2013).

E21.13 Vodcasts/vidcasts

Video podcasts – called vodcasts or vidcasts – can be viewed on the internet or downloaded for later viewing. So that readers can locate the original, cite and reference where you obtained the vodcast.

Citation order:

- Author
- Year that the site was published/last updated (in round brackets)
- Title of vodcast (in italics)
- [Vodcast]
- Available at: URL
- (Accessed: date)

Example

In-text citation

The vodcast (Walker and Carruthers, 2008) explained the proposal.

Reference list

Walker, A. and Carruthers, S. (2008) *Storage on your network* [Vodcast]. Available at: http://www.labrats.tv/episodes/ep126.html (Accessed: 19 June 2015).

E21.14 Microform (microfiche and microfilm)

Citation order:

- Author
- Year of publication (in round brackets)
- Title of microform (in italics)
- Medium (in square brackets)
- Place of publication: publisher

Example

In-text citation

Data from Fritsch (1987) …

Reference list

Fritsch, F.E. (1987) *The Fritsch collection: algae illustrations on microfiche* [Microfiche]. Ambleside: Freshwater Biological Association.

E22 Interviews

Citation order:

- Name of person interviewed
- Year of interview (in round brackets)
- Title of the interview (if any) (in single quotation marks)
- Interview with Interviewee
- Interviewed by Interviewer's name
- for Title of publication or broadcast (in italics)
- Day and month of interview, page numbers (if relevant)

> **Example: newspaper interview**
>
> `In-text citation`
>
> Riley (2008) believed that 'imagination has to be captured by reality'.
>
> `Reference list`
>
> Riley, B. (2008) 'The life of Riley'. Interview with Bridget Riley. Interviewed by Jonathan Jones for *The Guardian*, 5 July, p. 33.

> **Example: television interview**
>
> `In-text citation`
>
> The prime minister avoided the question (Blair, 2003).
>
> `Reference list`
>
> Blair, A. (2003) Interviewed by Jeremy Paxman for *Newsnight*, BBC Two Television, 2 February.

If published on the internet add:

- Available at: URL
- (Accessed: date)

> **Example: internet interview**
>
> `In-text citation`
>
> The President appeared confident in the discussion (Obama, 2015).
>
> `Reference list`
>
> Obama, B. (2015) Interviewed by Jon Sopel for *BBC News*, 24 July. Available at: http://www.bbc.co.uk/news/world-us-canada-33646543 (Accessed: 16 September 2015).

E23 Public communications

These include lectures, seminars, webinars, *PowerPoint* presentations, videoconferences/electronic discussion groups, bulletin boards/press releases, announcements/leaflets, advertisements/display boards, minutes of meetings and RSS feeds.

NB For communications in virtual learning environments, see Section E6.

E23.1 Lectures/seminars/webinars/*PowerPoint* presentations/videoconferences

Citation order:

- Author/speaker
- Year (in round brackets)
- Title of communication (in italics)
- Medium (in square brackets)
- Module code: module title (in italics) (if known)
- Institution
- Day/month

> **Example**
>
> **In-text citation**
>
> Points of interest from the lecture (Brown, 2016) …
>
> **Reference list**
>
> Brown, T. (2016) *Contemporary furniture* [Lecture to BSc Design Year 4], *DE816: Design for Industry*. Northumbria University. 21 April.

If referencing an *online communication*, use the following citation order:

- Author
- Year (in round brackets)
- Title of communication (in italics)
- Medium (in square brackets)
- Available at: URL
- (Accessed: date)

> **Example**
>
> **In-text citation**
>
> The excellent presentation (Schott, 2015) …
>
> **Reference list**
>
> Schott, H. (2015) *Biodiversity in North Wales* [*PowerPoint* presentation]. Available at: http://www.biodiverseviews.org.uk/nwales2 (Accessed: 16 August 2015).

E23.2 Electronic discussion groups and bulletin boards

NB For personal email correspondence, see Section E24. The examples in Sections E23.2–3 deal with email correspondence made public in electronic conferences, discussion groups and bulletin boards.

Citation order:

- Author of message
- Year of message (in round brackets)
- Subject of the message (in single quotation marks)
- Discussion group or bulletin board (in italics)
- Date posted: day/month
- Available email: email address

> **Example**
>
> **In-text citation**
>
> Debt cancellation was discussed by Peters (2015) …
>
> **Reference list**
>
> Peters, W.R. (2015) 'International finance questions', *British Business School Librarians Group discussion list*, 11 March. Available email: lisbusiness@ jiscmail.com.

E23.3 Entire discussion groups or bulletin boards

Citation order:

- List name (in italics)
- Year of last update (in round brackets)
- Available email: email address
- (Accessed: date)

> **Example**
>
> **In-text citation**
>
> The *Photography news list* (2015) …
>
> **Reference list**
>
> *Photography news list* (2015). Available email: pnl@btinfonet (Accessed: 3 April 2016).

E23.4 Press releases/ announcements

Citation order:

- Author/organisation
- Year issued (in round brackets)
- Title of communication (in italics)
- [Press release]
- Day/month

If available online, add:
- Available at: URL
- (Accessed: date)

> **Example**
>
> **In-text citation**
> This development (Google Inc., 2012) offered …
>
> **Reference list**
> Google Inc. (2012) *Google Maps heads north … way north* [Press release]. 23 August. Available at: http://www.google.com/intl/en/press/ (Accessed: 13 January 2016).

E23.5 Leaflets

By their nature, leaflets are unlikely to have all the citation/reference elements, so include as much information as possible. It may also be useful to include a copy of the leaflet in an appendix to your assignment.

Citation order:
- Author (individual or corporate)
- Date (if available – in round brackets)
- Title (in italics)
- [Leaflet obtained …]
- Date obtained

> **Example**
>
> **In-text citation**
> Lloyds TSB Bank plc (no date) provides insurance for its mortgages.
>
> **Reference list**
> Lloyds TSB Bank plc (no date) *Mortgages*. [Leaflet obtained in Paisley branch], 4 June 2015.

E23.6 Advertisements

If referencing information in an advertisement, you will need to specify where it was seen. This might be online, in a newspaper, on television or in a location. Advertisements are often short-lived, so it is important to include the date you viewed them.

Citation order:
- Cite and reference according to the medium in which the advertisement appeared (see examples)

> **Examples**
>
> **In-text citation**
> Advertisements by British Telecom (2015), Lloyds TSB (2015) and Northern Electric (2015) and that for the WOMAD festival in *The Guardian* (2015) …
>
> **Reference list**
> **Television advertisement**
> British Telecom (2015) *Office relocation gremlins* [Advertisement on ITV1 Television]. 23 November.
>
> **Newspaper advertisement**
> *The Guardian* (2015) 'WOMAD festival' [Advertisement]. 14 January, p. 12.
>
> **Internet advertisement**
> Lloyds TSB Bank plc (2015) *Selling your house?* [Advertisement]. Available at http://www.hotmail.com (Accessed: 13 February 2015).
>
> **Billboard advertisement**
> Northern Electric plc (2015) *Green energy* [Billboard at Ellison Road, Dunston-on-Tyne]. 14 January.

E23.7 Display boards, for example in museums

It is very rare for an author to be given for information on display boards, so the example uses the title first.

Citation order:
- Title (in italics)
- Year of production (if available – in round brackets)

- Display board at
- Name of venue, city
- Date observed

Example

In-text citation

Martin's vivid colours are a noted feature of his work (*Paintings of John Martin*, 2011).

Reference list

Paintings of John Martin (2011) Display board at Laing Art Gallery exhibition, Newcastle upon Tyne, 23 April 2013.

E23.8   Minutes of meetings

Citation order:

- Author (individual or group if identified)
- Year of meeting (in round brackets)
- Item being referenced (in single quotation marks)
- Title and date of meeting (in italics)
- Organisation
- Location of meeting

Example: with author identified

In-text citation

Jones (2013) suggested work shadowing and mentoring.

Reference list

Jones, T. (2013) 'Item 3.1: Developing our staff'. *Minutes of staff development committee meeting 23 February 2013*, Western Health Trust, Shrewsbury.

Example: with group name

In-text citation

The staff development committee (2013) suggested work shadowing and mentoring.

Reference list

Staff development committee (2013) 'Item 3.1: Developing our staff'. *Minutes of staff development committee meeting 23 February 2013*, Western Health Trust, Shrewsbury.

E23.9   RSS feeds

Rich Site Summary (RSS) is a method of notifying subscribers, through 'feeds', when a favourite web page such as a news source has been updated. You should reference the details of the original source, for example news web page, blog or newly published journal article, not the RSS feed.

Citation order:

- Author/organisation
- Year issued (in round brackets)
- Title of communication (in italics)
- [RSS]
- Day/month

If available online add:

- Available at: URL
- (Accessed: date)

Example

The library extension was completed in April 2012 (Durham University Library, 2012).

Durham University Library (2012) *Library east wing opens* [RSS] 23 April. Available at: https://www.dur.ac.uk/feeds/news/?section=14 (Accessed: 25 April 2015).

E24 Personal communications

NB For phonecasts, see Section E21.11.

Personal communications via conversation, phone, *Skype*, *FaceTime*, email, text message, letter or fax can be referenced as follows.

Citation order:

* Sender/speaker/author
* Year of communication (in round brackets)
* Medium of communication
* Receiver of communication
* Day/month of communication

Examples

This was disputed by Walters (2015).

Walters, F. (2015) Conversation with John Stephens, 13 August.

Walters, F. (2015) Letter to John Stephens, 23 January.

Walters, F. (2015) Email to John Stephens, 14 August.

Walters, F. (2015) Telephone conversation with John Stephens, 25 December.

Walters, F. (2015) *Skype* conversation with John Stephens, 21 June.

Walters, F. (2015) *FaceTime* conversation with John Stephens, 21 June.

Walters, F. (2015) Text message to John Stephens, 14 June.

Walters, F. (2015) Fax to John Stephens, 17 December.

Note that both the in-text citations and references begin with the name of the sender of the communication (for letters, emails, texts or faxes).

NB You may need to seek permission from other parties in the correspondence before quoting them in your work. You might also include a copy of written communications in your appendices, or note where the communication/correspondence can be located ('library', for example).

E25 Genealogical sources

Use the name of the person(s) and the date of the event as the in-text citation and provide the full details in the reference list.

E25.1 Birth, marriage and death certificates

Citation order:

- Name of person (in single quotation marks)
- Year of event (in round brackets)
- Certified copy of … certificate for … (in italics)
- Full name of person (forenames, surname) (in italics)
- Day/month/year of event (in italics)
- Application number from certificate
- Location of Register Office

If you retrieved the certificate online, after application number from certificate, add:

- Year of last update (in round brackets)
- Available at: URL
- (Accessed: date)

> **Example**
>
> **In-text citation**
> Amy was born in Bristol ('Amy Jane Bennett', 1874) …
>
> **Reference list**
> 'Amy Jane Bennett' (1874) *Certified copy of birth certificate for Amy Jane Bennett, 10 April 1874*. Application number 4001788/C. Bristol Register Office.

E25.2 Wills

Citation order:

- Title of document (in italics)
- Year of will (in round brackets)
- Name of archive or repository
- Reference number

> **Example**
>
> **In-text citation**
> Doubleday's nephews inherited his estates (*Will of Michael Doubleday of Alnwick Abbey, Northumberland*, 1797).
>
> **Reference list**
> *Will of Michael Doubleday of Alnwick Abbey, Northumberland* (1797) The National Archives: Public Record Office. Catalogue reference: PROB/11/1290.

E25.3 Censuses

Citation order:

- Name of person (in single quotation marks)
- Year of census (in round brackets)
- Census return for … (in italics)
- Street, place, county (in italics)
- Registration subdistrict (in italics)
- Public Record Office:
- Piece number, folio number, page number

If you retrieved the information online, add:

- Year of last update (in round brackets)
- Available at: URL
- (Accessed: date)

In-text citation

Thomas Wilson moved to Willington in the 1850s ('Thomas Wilson', 1861).

Reference list

'Thomas Wilson' (1861) *Census return for New Row, Willington, St Oswald subdistrict, County Durham.* Public Record Office: PRO RG9/3739, folio 74, p. 11 (2008). Available at: http://www.ancestry.co.uk (Accessed: 23 July 2015).

E25.4 Parish registers

Citation order:

- Name of person (in single quotation marks)
- Year of event (in round brackets)
- Baptism, marriage or burial of …
- Full name of person (forenames, surname)
- Day/month/year of event
- Title of register (in italics)

If you retrieved the certificate online, add:

- Year of last update (in round brackets)
- Available at: URL
- (Accessed: date)

Example

In-text citation

Mary and Edward's wedding ('Edward Robson and Mary Slack', 1784) …

Reference list

'Edward Robson and Mary Slack' (1784) Marriage of Edward Robson and Mary Slack, 6 May 1784. *St Augustine's Church Alston, Cumberland marriage register 1784–1812* (2004). Available at: http://www.genuki.org.uk/big/eng/CUL/Alston/MALS1701.html (Accessed: 13 July 2015).

E25.5 Military records

Citation order:

- Name of person (in single quotation marks)
- Year of publication (in round brackets)
- Title of publication (in italics)
- Publication details

If you retrieved the document online, add:

- Available at: URL
- (Accessed: date)

Example

In-text citation

Private Wakenshaw fought on even after losing his arm ('Adam Herbert Wakenshaw VC', 2008).

Reference list

'Adam Herbert Wakenshaw VC' (2008) *Commonwealth War Graves Commission casualty details.* Available at: http://www.cwgc.org/search/casualty_details.aspx?casualty=2212745 (Accessed: 21 June 2015).

E26 Manuscripts

E26.1 Individual manuscripts

If the author of a manuscript is known, use the following citation order:

- Author
- Year (in round brackets)
- Title of manuscript (in italics)
- Date (if available)
- Name of collection containing manuscript and reference number
- Location of manuscript in archive or repository

Example

In-text citation

The architect enjoyed a close relationship with his patron (Newton, 1785).

Reference list

Newton, W. (1785) *Letter to William Ord, 23 June*. Ord Manuscripts 324 E11/4, Northumberland Archives, Woodhorn.

Where the author of a manuscript is not known, use the following citation order:

- Title of manuscript (in italics)
- Year (if known, in round brackets)
- Name of collection containing manuscript and reference number
- Location of manuscript in archive or repository

Example

In-text citation

Expenditure was high in this period (*Fenham journal*, 1795).

Reference list

Fenham journal (1795) Ord Manuscripts, 324 E12, Northumberland Archives, Woodhorn.

E26.2 Collections of manuscripts

To refer to a whole collection of manuscripts (MS), use the name of the collection.

Citation order:

- Location of collection in archive or repository
- Name of collection

Example

In-text citation

Consulting the family records (British Library, Lansdowne MS), the author discovered ...

Reference list

British Library, Lansdowne MS.

Note that no date is given for a collection in the text or in the reference list as the collection contains items of various dates.

Section F
American Psychological Association (APA) referencing style

The APA referencing style is used in some social science subjects. Like Harvard, it uses an author-date format to identify the citation in the text. Full details are given in an alphabetical list of references.

Conventions when using the APA referencing style

Reference list layout

- All lines after the first line of each reference list entry should be indented half an inch from the left margin. This is called hanging indentation.

> **Example**
>
> Harris, P. H. (2016). *The freedom of information and the right to access personal data in Britain*. London: Freedom Press.

Authors/editors

- Authors' and editors' names are inverted (last name first). Give the last name (surname/family name) and initials
- Full stops are used after each of the author initials and spaces are inserted between initials
- Full stops are used after corporate names
- For editor or editors use the abbreviation Ed. or Eds., respectively, in round brackets.

> **Example**
>
> Brooks, G. J., & Gibbons, L. (Eds.).

Note the punctuation: ampersand (&) is used for 'and'; full stop after (Eds.).

Multiple authors and et al.

- For works with one or two authors include all names in every **in-text citation**; for works with three, four or five authors include all names in the first in-text citation and then abbreviate to the first author name plus et al. (not italicised) for subsequent citations; and for works with six or more authors abbreviate to the first author name plus et al. for all in-text citations
- For your **reference list**, give all authors *up to seven*, with the last author name preceded by an ampersand (&). Where you have *more than seven authors*, you should list the *first six* then use an ellipsis (…) and list the name of the last author of the work (no ampersand is required).

> **Example: work with five authors**
>
> **In-text citation**
>
> Games can assist recovery (Weathers et al., 2014) …
>
> **Reference list**
>
> Weathers, L., Bedell, J. R., Marlowe, H., Gordon, R. E., & Adams, J. (2014). Using psychotherapeutic games to train patients' skills. In R. E. Gordon and K. K. Gordon (Eds.) *Systems of treatment for the mentally ill* (pp. 109–124). New York, NY: Grune & Stratton.

Year of publication

- In brackets, followed by a full stop, for example (2016).

Titles

- The titles of sources are italicised, as are volume numbers of journal articles, but not issue or page numbers
- For a book, only the first letter of the first word of the title and subtitle (if there is one) and any **proper nouns** are capitalised
- Full stops are inserted after book titles

> **Example**
>
> *Psychoanalysis: Its image and its public in China.*

- Titles of articles within journals, or chapters within books, are not enclosed in quotation marks.
- For journal titles, each major word of the title is capitalised and followed by a comma

> **Example**
>
> *Journal of Comparative and Physiological Psychology,*

Editions

- Edition is abbreviated to ed. and enclosed in round brackets, with a full stop after the brackets (6th ed.).

- With the exception of first editions, edition number is included after the title in round brackets. Note that there is no full stop after the title before the round brackets.

> **Example**
>
> Ramage, P. L. (2016). *History in the making* (4th ed.). London: Harvest Press.

Place of publication

- For place of publication, you should always list the city and US state, using the two-letter abbreviation without full stops – for example New York, NY. Spell out the country names if outside the UK or the USA – for example Melbourne, Australia.

Issue information for periodicals

- Volume numbers are italicised.

Page numbers

- Page numbers for book chapters are given immediately after the title of the book in round brackets and before publication details
- Unlike other periodicals (journals and magazines), p. or pp. precedes page numbers for a newspaper reference in APA style.

Internet sources

- In APA the word Internet is always capitalised, whereas website is not
- Internet sources should be indicated by Retrieved from URL, or doi:

Note that APA style does not include a retrieval date for online sources

- APA also states that it is not necessary to include the name of the database when referencing online journals or ebook collections

- No punctuation marks are added after DOIs or URLs in reference list entries.

Footnotes and endnotes

- APA does not generally recommend the use of footnotes and endnotes. However, if you still need to provide explanatory notes for your work, you should use a **superscript number** following almost any punctuation marks. Footnote numbers should not follow hyphens, and if they appear in a sentence in brackets, the footnote number should be inserted within the brackets.

Example

Researchers believe that the occurrence of dementia in England points to a number of highly pertinent facts.[1] (These have now been published separately.[2])

Secondary (Indirect) sources

It is always better to read the original or primary sources so that you can reference them fully, but sometimes this is difficult. The APA *Publication manual* advises that you should 'use secondary sources sparingly, for instance, when the original work is out of print, unavailable through usual sources, or not available in English' (American Psychological Association, 2009, p. 178). In such a case, you would need to cite the original or primary source in the text of your work, the secondary source in round brackets (parentheses) and provide a full reference in the reference list for the secondary source.

Example

Hislop (as cited in Richards, 2013, p. 56) argued that …

Thus, only the details for Richards' work would appear in your reference list (unless you were able to read Hislop's work, then you could also include these details in your reference list).

How to reference common sources

F1   Books

Citation order:
- Author/Editor (surname followed by initials)
- Year of publication (in round brackets)
- Title (in italics)
- Edition (only include the edition number if it is not the first edition)
- Place of publication: publisher

Example

In-text citation

Earlier analysis (Freud, 1936, p. 54) …

Reference list

Freud, A. (1936). *The ego and the mechanisms of defense*. New York, NY: International Universities Press.

F2   Chapters/sections of edited books

Citation order:
- Author of the chapter/section (surname followed by initials)
- Year of publication (in round brackets)
- Title of chapter/section
- In
- Name of editor of book (Ed.)
- Title of book (in italics)
- Page numbers of chapter/section (in round brackets)
- Place of publication: publisher

Example

`In-text citation`

The view proposed by Leites (2013, p. 444) …

`Reference list`

Leites, N. (2013). Transference interpretations only? In A. H. Esman (Ed.) *Essential papers on transference* (pp. 434–454). New York, NY: New York University Press.

F3 Anthologies

Whole, edited anthologies should be referenced like any other whole edited book would be. Only the editor appears in the author part of the reference.

Citation order:

- Editor (surname followed by initials) (Ed.)
- Year (in round brackets)
- Title (in italics)
- Place of publication: publisher

OR if viewed online:

- doi: or Retrieved from URL

Example: print anthology

`In-text citation`

… in the work (Hollings, 2013).

`Reference list`

Hollings, P. (Ed.). (2013). *The complete works of Henry Rawlings* (Vol. 3). London: Literary Minds.

Example: online anthology

`In-text citation`

… in the work (Hollings, 2013).

`Reference list`

Hollings, P. (Ed.). (2013). *The complete works of Henry Rawlings* (Vol. 3). Retrieved from http://books.google.com/books

To reference multiple volumes in an anthology, include the range of years over which the volumes were published (unless all were published in the same year) and the volume numbers in round brackets after the title.

Example: print

`In-text citation`

More recent studies (Farrow & Morgan, 2009–2012) …

`Reference list`

Farrow, P. S., & Morgan, L. (Eds.). (2009–2012). *Homeopathic medicine: A history and study* (Vols. 1–4). Lancaster: Pear Tree Books.

Example: online

`In-text citation`

More recent studies (Farrow & Morgan, 2009–2012) …

`Reference list`

Farrow, P. S., & Morgan, L. (Eds.). (2009–2012). *Homeopathic medicine: A history and study* (Vols. 1–4). Retrieved from http://www.amazon.co.uk/Kindle-eBooks-books/b?ie=UTF8&node=341689031

F4 Translated works

Citation order:

- Author/Editor (surname followed by initials)
- Year of publication (in round brackets)
- Title (in italics)
- Name of translator, Trans. (in round brackets)
- Place of publication: publisher

F5   Book reviews

Citation order:

- Reviewer (surname followed by initials)
- Year of publication (in round brackets)
- Title of book review
- [Review of the book *Title of book*, by Author of book]
- Title of serial where the review appears (in italics)
- Volume number (in italics)
- Issue (in round brackets), page numbers
- doi: or Retrieved from URL (if viewed online)

If the review is untitled, use the text in square brackets as the title; retain the brackets to indicate that the material is a description of form and content, not a title.

You can use this format for any reviews; simply indicate the medium being reviewed in the brackets (film, DVD, television programme …).

If the reviewed item is a film, DVD or other medium, include the year of release after the title of the work, separated by a comma.

F6   Ebooks

Citation order:

- Author/Editor (surname followed by initials)
- Year of publication (in round brackets)
- Title (in italics)
- doi: or Retrieved from URL

Mobile ebook formats

To reference Kindle or other mobile device ebook formats you must include the following information: the author, date of publication, title, ebook version and, instead of publisher details, use either the book's **digital object identifier (DOI)** or, if no DOI, the place where you downloaded the book.

In your text, however, citing a specific quotation can become confusing because ebooks often lack page numbers (though PDF versions may have them). Kindle books have 'location' numbers and % marks which are static, but those are of no use to anyone who does not have a Kindle, or is using a different font-size display. So, to cite a quotation or section in text, follow APA's guidelines for direct quotations of online material, using the major sections (chapter, section and paragraph number; abbreviate if titles are long), as you would do if you were citing the Bible or Shakespeare. In general, provide as much information as the reader needs to locate the material you are using.

Example

In-text citation

One of the main points of his argument (Carmichael, 2014, Chapter 4, Section 3, para. 2) …

Reference list

Carmichael, B. (2014). *Inheritance* [Kindle version]. Retrieved from http://www. amazon.co.uk

---

F7 Journal articles

Citation order:

- Author (surname followed by initials)
- Year of publication (in round brackets)
- Title of article
- Title of journal (in italics)
- Volume number (in italics)
- Issue (in round brackets)
- Page numbers

Example

In-text citation

Research by Frosch (2012) …

Reference list

Frosch, A. (2012). Transference: Psychic reality and material reality. *Psychoanalytic Psychology, 19*(4), 603–633.

F8 Ejournal articles

Citation order:

- Author (surname followed by initials)
- Year of publication (in round brackets)
- Title of article

- Title of journal (in italics)
- Volume number (in italics)
- Issue (in round brackets), page numbers
- doi: or Retrieved from URL

Example

In-text citation

Violence is a factor in many instances of transference (Shubs, 2014).

Reference list

Shubs, C. H. (2014). Transference issues concerning victims of violent crime and other traumatic incidents of adulthood. *Psychoanalytic Psychology, 25*(1), 122–141. doi: 10.1037/0736-9735.25.1.122

F9 Magazine/newspaper/ newsletter articles

Dates for magazines, newspapers and newsletters should include the year and the exact date of the publication (month or month and day). This means that the month should be given for monthlies, and the month and day for weeklies and dailies. If the magazine uses a season with the year, put the year, a comma, and the season in parentheses (2014, Winter).

Citation order:

- Author (surname followed by initials)
- Year and date of publication (in round brackets)
- Title of article
- Title of magazine/newspaper/newsletter (in italics)
- Volume number (in italics) – if available
- Issue (in round brackets) – if available
- Page numbers – if available
- doi: or Retrieved from URL (if required)

NB APA style requires the use of p., or pp. for specifying pages in a **newspaper**

reference (see the example). Their use is not required in other periodicals.

Example: print magazine article

Harrison, L. E. (2014, November 23). The return of the trains. *Cumbria Times*, 54–56.

Example: print newspaper article

Vardy, A. (2014, November 23). New treatments for travel sickness. *The Independent*, pp. 16–17.

Example: online article

Burroughs, S. (2013, Autumn). How to create a dynamic website. *Website Design, 89.* Retrieved from http://www.websdesign.com/articles/createdynweb

---

F10   Prepublication journal articles

F10.1   Draft manuscripts

A manuscript for an article that is still in draft form can be cited and referenced using the year the draft was written.

Example

In-text citation

… in her latest research (Morgan, 2015).

Reference list

Morgan, P. R. (2015). *Hierarchies in the bee world: A field study.* Manuscript in preparation.

F10.2   Manuscripts submitted for publication

If a manuscript has been submitted for publication, use the year it was written, not the year it was submitted, as the date.

Example

In-text citation

This cutting-edge research (Hastings, 2015) …

Reference list

Hastings, P. L. (2015). *Combined therapy: Medication, talking therapies and self-help in the treatment of anxiety and depression.* Manuscript submitted for publication.

If the article is accepted for publication, the status changes to *in press* and the name of the journal can be included in the reference.

Example

In-text citation

This new research (Hastings, in press) …

Reference list

Hastings, P. L. (in press). Combined therapy: Medication, talking therapies and self-help in the treatment of anxiety and depression. *Mental Illness Quarterly.*

F10.3   Advance online publications

Citation order
- Author (surname followed by initials)
- Year of posting (in round brackets)
- Title of the article
- Journal title (in italics)
- Advance online publication
- doi of the journal's home page or Retrieved from URL

Example

In-text citation

The latest research (Hastings, 2015) …

Reference list

Hastings, P. L. (2015). Combined therapy: Medication, talking therapies and self-help in the treatment of anxiety and depression. *Mental Illness Quarterly*. Advance online publication. doi: 15.1098/a00045361

F11   Conferences and symposia

F11.1   Full conference proceedings (print or electronic)

Citation order:

- Author/Editor (surname, followed by initials)
- Year of publication (in round brackets)
- Title of conference: Subtitle of conference (in italics)
- Location, date of conference (in italics)
- Place of publication: publisher

OR if viewed online:

- doi: or Retrieved from URL

Example

In-text citation

… in the full conference proceedings (Hewlett & Carson, 2015).

Reference list

Hewlett, P., & Carson, L. (Eds.). (2015). *Preparing nurses for the next decade: Proceedings of the National Conference on Education in Nursing, University of Cumbria, 2014.* Lancaster: Greendale Press.

F11.2   Conference papers in print proceedings

Citation order:

- Author of paper
- Year, month, date of paper (in round brackets)
- Title of paper
- In
- Editors (if required)
- Title of published proceedings (in italics)
- Paper presented at
- Title of conference: Subtitle of conference
- Location of conference
- Page numbers (in round brackets)
- Place of publication: publisher

Example

In-text citation

In their expert analysis (Peters, T., & Richards, K., 2013) …

Reference list

Peters, T., & Richards, K. (2013). Refugees or asylum seekers: How will Europe respond? In M. Dibbs, L. Williams, & S. Hussein (Eds.), *Europe's role in the midst of international crises*. Paper presented at the Proceedings of the 5th International Conference on Human Rights, Geneva, Switzerland (pp. 145–167). Geneva, Switzerland: Jungfrau Press.

F11.3   Conference papers from the Internet

Citation order:

- Author of paper
- Year (in round brackets)
- Title of paper (in italics)
- Paper presented at
- Title of conference: Subtitle of conference

- Location of conference
- doi: or Retrieved from URL

> **Example**
>
> **In-text citation**
>
> A recent study (Dawson, 2015) ...
>
> **Reference list**
>
> Dawson, H. (2015). *Is Alzheimer's a transmissible disease?* Paper presented at the WHO Symposium on Dementia, Geneva, Switzerland. doi: 15.1243/GH.2015.132

F12 Government publications

Citation order:
- Name of government department
- Year of publication (in round brackets)
- Title (in italics)
- Report series and number (in round brackets)
- Place of publication: publisher

OR if viewed online:
- doi: or Retrieved from URL

> **Example**
>
> **In-text citation**
>
> Government policy on energy reduction (Department for Energy & Climate Change, 2014) ...
>
> **Reference list**
>
> Department for Energy & Climate Change. (2014). *Community Energy Strategy* (URN 14D/019). Retrieved from https://www.gov.uk/government/publications/community-energy-strategy

For *Command Papers* (including *Green* and *White Papers*) insert the paper number after the title in round brackets.

> **Examples**
>
> Department for Education. (2015). *Government response to the Education Select Committee report: Extremism in schools – the Trojan Horse affair.* (Cm. 9094). London: Her Majesty's Stationery Office.
>
> OR if viewed online:
>
> Department for Education. (2015). *Government response to the Education Select committee report: Extremism in schools – the Trojan Horse affair.* (Cm. 9094). Retrieved from https://www.gov.uk/government/publications/extremism-in-schools-response-to-education-select-committee

If you are referencing government publications from more than one country, add the country after the department name, for example Department of Energy (USA) and Department for Education (UK).

F13 Research reports

Research and technical reports form part of the larger body of publications known as grey literature: material that is produced by government, academics, business and industry in print and electronic formats, but which is not controlled by commercial publishers.

Citation order for online reports:
- Author (surname followed by initials)
- Year of publication (in round brackets)
- Title of report (in italics)
- doi: or Retrieved from URL

Example

In-text citation

Charnley (2015) highlights the importance …

Reference list

Charnley, S. (2015). *The historical significance of religious iconography.* Retrieved from http://www.religioncounts.govt.nz/data/assets/pdf_file/0024/3693.pdf

For printed reports by corporate authors where they are also the publisher you would substitute 'Author' for the publisher.

Example

In-text citation

… in their report (International Labour Organization, 2014).

Reference list

International Labour Organization. (2014). *Equality at work: Tackling new challenges.* Geneva, Switzerland: Author.

F14 Theses and dissertations

Citation order:

- Author (surname followed by initials)
- Year of submission (in round brackets)
- Title of dissertation/thesis (in italics)
- Degree statement (in round brackets)
- Degree-awarding body, location

Example

In-text citation

Research by Brodie (2013) …

Reference list

Brodie, L. M. (2013). *Speciality regional foods in the UK: an investigation from the perspectives of marketing and social history* (Unpublished PhD thesis). Newcastle University, Newcastle upon Tyne.

F15 Organisation or personal Internet sites

Citation order:

- Author
- Year the site was published/last updated (in round brackets)
- Title of Internet site (with format in brackets if necessary, for example for a blog)
- doi: or Retrieved from URL

Example: organisation

In-text citation

There are several career paths (British Psychological Association, 2012) …

Reference list

British Psychological Association. (2012). How to become a psychologist. Retrieved from http://www.bps.org.uk/careers-education-training/how-become-psychologist/how-become-psychologist

Example: personal

In-text citation

As suggested by one website (Black, 2016) …

Reference list

Black, J. B. (2016). Learn to profile people. Retrieved from http://lifehacker.com/346372/learn-to-profile-people

Below are examples of web pages where pieces of information are not available.

Remember, you should always question the validity of sources where crucial elements are missing in order to establish the academic credibility of the source.

F15.1 Web pages with no authors

Use the title of the web page as the first element in the citation and reference.

The in-text citation uses double quotation marks around the title or abbreviated title.

Note that month and date are also given in the reference list.

> **Example**
>
> **In-text citation**
>
> ("Randall's spectacular production," 2015) …
>
> **Reference list**
>
> Randall's spectacular production has now been running for three years. (2015, February 17). Retrieved from http:// www.msnbc.msn.com/id/569876409/ ns/arts_news/

F15.2 Web pages with no authors or titles

In the reference list you should substitute a description of the document inside square brackets.

> **Example**
>
> **In-text citation**
>
> … the document (Map of the world, 1644).
>
> **Reference list**
>
> [Map of the world]. (1644). Retrieved from http://www.cartographslibrary/236784/ 17cent/

F15.3 Web pages with no date

Use the abbreviation n.d. for no date.

> **Example**
>
> **In-text citation**
>
> … of its history (Rydwell School, n.d.).
>
> **Reference list**
>
> Rydwell School. (n.d.). History of the school. Retrieved from http://www. educ/about/schoolhistory/index

F16 Blogs

Citation order:

- Author (surname followed by initials)
- Year and date of post (in round brackets)
- Title of post
- [Blog post]
- Retrieved from URL

> **Example**
>
> **In-text citation**
>
> The disconcerting comments (Haynes, 2015) …
>
> **Reference list**
>
> Haynes, R. (2015, March 18). Global warming warnings [Blog post]. Retrieved from http://globalnesslife. blogs.cfg.com/2015/3/18/global- warming-warnings/

F17   Wikis

Wikis are collaborative sites in which several (usually unidentified) authors can add and edit information. There have been instances of false information being presented, although wiki editors try to ensure that the information is correct. Nevertheless, many tutors specifically prohibit students from citing *Wikipedia*. *Wikipedia* is not a scholarly resource but there are times when it can provide a useful starting point or definition of a topic. In APA wikis are referenced in the same way as an entry in an online reference work. The retrieval date is always required because the source material may change over time.

Citation order:
- Title of article
- (n.d.).
- In
- Title of wiki (in italics)
- Retrieved date and from

Example

In-text citation

Homeopathy is a system of alternative medicine (Homeopathy, n.d.).

Reference list

Homeopathy. (n.d.). In *Wikipedia*. Retrieved September 19, 2015, from https:// en.wikipedia.org/wiki/ Homeopathy

F18   Social media

There are three main ways to cite social media content in the APA style:
- generally with a URL
- as a personal communication
- with a typical APA style in-text citation and reference list entry. If you discuss in a general way any website or page, it is sufficient to give the URL in the text the first time it is mentioned. *No reference list entry is needed*.

Example

In-text citation

Health agencies such as NICE provide advice and guidance to improve health and social care on their website (https:// www.nice.org.uk).

If you paraphrase or quote specific, retrievable information from social media, provide an in-text citation (with the author and date) and a reference list entry (with the author, date, title, and source URL).

Specific examples for Twitter and Facebook are given below.

Note that hashtags # are a common sight on Twitter and Facebook and other platforms, and you may ask how you cite and reference them. The answer is that you do not. This is because, just like your research on a database, finding and searching with the right hashtag is part of your research methodology. So, you can simply describe it in your text, for example, "During the recent migrant crisis in Europe I searched Facebook and Twitter for the hashtags #refugees, #migrants and #asylumseekers appearing between September 1, 2015 and October 15, 2015". Your reader can then try to replicate the search if they wish to follow your evidence. To refer to any tweets or posts that you find on the sites, you should reference them as shown in the relevant examples below.

See also the Instagram example in section F23.2 Photographs from the Internet.

F18.1   Twitter

On Twitter, provide the author's screen name in square brackets (if only the screen name is known, provide it without brackets).

Note that titles of tweets, status updates or photographs are not italicised: items that stand alone, like videos and photo albums, are italicised.

Citation order:

- Author (surname followed by initials) and/or [Screen name]
- Year, month day (in round brackets)
- Title of page
- [Tweet]
- Retrieved from URL

> **Example**
>
> **In-text citation**
>
> His ongoing message to Scotland … (Cameron, 2014).
>
> **Reference list**
>
> Cameron, D. [DavidCameron]. (2014, September 10). #Scotland United UK [Tweet]. Retrieved from https://twitter.com/DavidCameron/status/60789345

F18.2   Facebook

When the author is an individual, as well as providing initials, spell out his or her given name in square brackets.

Citation order:

- Author (surname followed by initials) and [given name in square brackets]
- Year, month, day (in round brackets)
- Title of page
- [Facebook status update]
- Retrieved from URL

> **Example**
>
> **In-text citation**
>
> The use of anti-depressants for new mothers … (Sissons, 2014)
>
> **Reference list**
>
> Sissons, H. [Hilary]. (2014, April 18). The range of medication prescribed for new mums suffering from postnatal depression … [Facebook status update]. Retrieved from https://www.facebook.com/hilarysissons/posts/103567529148

F19   Film or video recordings

Citation order:

- Name of director (surname followed by initials)
- (Director) &
- Name of producer (surname followed by initials)
- (Producer)
- Year of distribution (in round brackets)
- Title (in italics)
- [Medium]
- Place of distribution: distributor

> **Example**
>
> **In-text citation**
>
> Jackson (2014) cleverly demonstrates …
>
> **Reference list**
>
> Jackson, P. (Director), & Cunningham, C., Weiner, Z., Walsh, F., & Jackson, P. (Producers). (2014). *The Hobbit: The desolation of Smaug* [DVD]. London: Warner Bros. Entertainment UK Ltd.

F20   Online videos (for example YouTube)

Citation order:

- Author (surname followed by initials) and/or [Screen name]

- Year, month day (in round brackets)
- Title of video (in italics)
- [Video file]
- doi: or Retrieved from URL

Example

In-text citation

He questioned the continuation of life on Earth (Rees, 2012).

Reference list

Rees, M. [TED]. (2012, April 15). *Sir Martin Rees: Earth in its final century?* [Video file]. Retrieved from http://www.youtube.com/watch?v=3qF26MbYgOA

To point the reader to a specific place in an audiovisual source, such as when you cite a **direct quotation**, include a timestamp (hour:minute:seconds) in the in-text citation, just as you would include a page number under similar circumstances for a print source such as a book or journal article.

Example

In-text citation

'The artefact showed all the signs of deliberate vandalism and led us to believe that …' (Harris, Golding, & Bagguley, 2014, 8:25).

Reference list

Harris, G., Golding, P., & Bagguley, L. M. (2014, March 24). *Understanding medieval church architecture in the south-eastern counties of England.* [Video file]. Retrieved from http://www.youtube.com/watch?a=5pG34NkYdWQ

F21 Sound/music recordings

Citation order:
- Artist/Songwriter (surname followed by initials)
- Copyright year (in round brackets)

- Title of song/recording
- [Recorded by artist if different from songwriter]
- On
- Title of album (in italics)
- [Medium of recording]
- Location: label
- Date of recording (if different from copyright date)

Example

In-text citation

… in his lyrics (Taupin, 1975).

Reference list

Taupin, B. (1975). Someone saved my life tonight [Recorded by Elton John]. On *Captain fantastic and the brown dirt cowboy* [CD]. London: Big Pig Music Limited.

F22 Musical scores (sheet music)

Citation order:
- Name of composer (surname followed by initials)
- (Composer)
- Date (in round brackets)
- Title of work (in italics)
- Place of publication: publisher

You may need to include other relevant information, such as librettist (see example), and you may need to provide more details in square brackets to identify for the reader which score you used.

Example

In-text citation

... Hollins & Simmons (2008).

Reference list

Hollins J. (Composer), & Simmons, J. D. (Librettist). (2008). *Giselda: An opera in two acts* [Score and parts]. Mainz, Germany: Schott Helicon.

If you are using something like a Dover reprint of an old score, there is no need to include the information about the original publishing company, but do include the original publication date.

NB When you cite a republished work, you should give both dates of publication.

Example

In-text citation

... (Mendelssohn, 1830/1999).

Reference list

Mendelssohn F. (1999). *The Hebrides.* London: Initial Music Publishing. (Original work published 1830).

F23 Visual arts (paintings, sculptures and installations)

APA provides advice on audiovisual media, but it focuses mostly on audio, video and television. There are no specific guidelines for paintings, sculptures or more complicated installations. So, follow the principle that a good reference should contain enough information to lead your reader to the source you used, as concisely and clearly as possible. At a minimum, this should include the artist's name, year(s) of production, title of the work, and any other necessary or relevant information such as the medium, and the location of the work.

Citation order:

- Artist (surname followed by initials)
- Year of production (in round brackets)
- Title of work (in italics)
- [Medium]
- Location of the work

Example

In-text citation

... his inspirational sculpture (Gormley, 1998).

Reference list

Gormley, A. (1998). *The angel of the north* [Sculpture]. Low Fell, Gateshead.

If you want to reference the work as seen on a website, you would use the website as the location element of your reference.

Example

Reference list

Gormley, A. (1998). *The angel of the north* [Sculpture]. Retrieved from http://www. newcastlegateshead.com/things-to-do/ the-angel-of-the-north-p26491

F23.1 Television broadcasts

Citation order:

- Writer (surname followed by initials)
- (Writer)
- &
- Director (surname followed by initials)
- (Director)
- Date of broadcast or copyright (in round brackets)
- Title of episode
- [Television series episode]
- In
- Producer (initials followed by surname)
- (Producer)
- Series title (in italics)
- Place of broadcast: broadcaster

Examples

In-text citation

… of their intriguing script (Roberts & Moffat, 2014).

Reference list

Roberts, G., & Moffat, S. (Writers), & Murphy, P. (Director). (2014, September 27). The caretaker [Television series episode]. In N. Wilson (Producer). *Doctor Who.* London: BBC.

F23.2 Photographs from the Internet

Citation order:

- Photographer (surname followed by initials)
- Year of production (in round brackets)
- Title of work (in italics)
- [Medium]
- Retrieved from URL

Example

In-text citation

His beautiful photograph (Kitto, 2015) …

Reference list

Kitto, J. (2015). *Golden sunset* [Photograph]. Retrieved from http:// www.jameskitto.co.uk/photo_1827786. html

If you wish to reference photographs or video files from a social media site such as Instagram (or Tumblr, Flickr and Pinterest) there are distinctions between the media to which you are referring. If you are referencing a photograph do not italicise the title. However, if you are referencing a photograph collection/album or video file do italicise the title.

Example: Instagram photograph

In-text citation

… the photograph (Nordeman, 2015).

Reference list

Nordeman, L. (2015). Kentucky derby [Photograph]. Retrieved from https:// instagram.com/tagged/photo_feature

Example: Instagram photograph collection or video file

In-text citation

Fisher's collection of deconstructed photographs (2016) …

Reference list

Fisher, D. (2016). *Deepbody* [Photo album]. Retrieved from https:// instagram.com/deepbody

F24 Personal communications

This includes information in formats that cannot be obtained by a reader, including unrecorded and unpublished interviews, conversations, emails and notes you make during lectures.

No personal communication is included in your reference list; instead, parenthetically cite the communicator's name, the phrase 'personal communication', and the date of the communication in your main text only.

Example

In-text citation

The email stated that the company accepted an error had been made (H. Thomas, personal communication, May 14, 2014).

F24.1 Published interviews

Published interviews should be cited according to the format in which you have used them: if you read the interview in a newspaper or magazine article, or if you watched the interview online (for example YouTube) use the appropriate citation order for that format.

> **Example**
>
> **In-text citation**
>
> Riley (2008) related her concerns …
>
> **Reference list**
>
> Riley, B. (2008, July 5). The life of Riley. Interview with Bridget Riley. Interviewed by Jonathan Jones for *The Guardian*, p. 33.

F24.2 Unpublished interviews

If you interviewed another person as part of your research, and they agreed to be quoted in your work, cite this as a personal communication in your text.

> **Example**
>
> **In-text citation**
>
> The Professor noted the important discoveries she made about memory loss (J. Wilkinson, personal communication, April 27, 2014).

Do not include this in your reference list because there is no copy of the information available for the reader to use.

If interviewees were speaking confidentially, do not include a citation.

> **Example**
>
> **In-text citation**
>
> Fourteen of the twenty interviewees expressed concerns about steroid use in teenagers.

F25 Datasets

Citation order:

- Author (surname followed by initials) or name of organisation
- Year of publication (in round brackets)
- Title (in italics)
- Report series and number (in round brackets)
- Retrieved from URL

> **Example**
>
> **In-text citation**
>
> Barley prices fell in January and February 2014 before a sharp increase in early March (Department for Environment, Food & Rural Affairs, 2014).
>
> **Reference list**
>
> Department for Environment, Food & Rural Affairs. (2014). Price series for cereals – weekly (Statistical Data Set Commodity Prices). Retrieved from https://www.gov.uk/government/statistical-data-sets/commodity-prices

Sample text

The following sample piece of text illustrates how various in-text sources would be included in APA style in your work.

Homeopathy is a system of alternative medicine (Homeopathy, n.d.) and its history is comprehensively documented in a multi-volume work (Farrow & Morgan, 2009–2012). However, for brief introductory studies of the subject, the recently published articles of Bradley (2015) and Harvey (2016) present excellent starting points and complement the seminal analysis by Carmichael (2014). A more dated government survey sheds light on the issue of evidence relating to the effectiveness of homeopathy (Department of Health, 2010), while one charity's website, promoting and campaigning for access for all, includes a great deal of interesting information, including testimonials (British Homeopathic Association, 2015).

Sample reference list

All sources are listed alphabetically. Note that the first line of the reference is not indented, but subsequent lines are, so that the authors' names are easily identifiable (see 'Reference list layout' at the beginning of Section F).

Bradley, C. H. (2015). Evidential issues concerning patients of homeopathy. *Psychoanalytic Psychology, 28*(4), 122–141. doi: 10.1037/0736-9735.25.1.122

British Homeopathic Association. (2015). Homeopathy – a healthcare choice for everyone. Retrieved from http://www.britishhomeopathic.org/

Carmichael, B. (2014). *Homeopathy* [Kindle version]. Retrieved from http://www.amazon.co.uk

Department of Health. (2010). *Government response to the Science and Technology Committee report 'Evidence Check 2: Homeopathy'*. Retrieved from https://www.gov.uk/government/publications/government-response/

Farrow, P. S. & Morgan, L. (Eds.). (2009–2012). *Homeopathic medicine: A history and study* (Vols. 1–4). Lancaster: Pear Tree Books.

Harvey, A. (2016). Homeopathy: New evidence for and against. *Medicine Today, 29*(4), 503–543.

Homeopathy. (n.d.). In *Wikipedia*. Retrieved September 19, 2015, from https://en.wikipedia.org/wiki/Homeopathy

For more information on using the APA referencing style, see:

American Psychological Association. (2009). *Publication manual of the American Psychological Association* (6th ed.). (Washington, DC: American Psychological Association).

American Psychological Association. (2012). *APA style guide to electronic references* (6th ed.). [Kindle edition]. Available at: http://www.amazon.co.uk/Style-Guide-Electronic-References-Edition-ebook/dp/B008674FW8

Two useful sources of further guidance on APA are the APA blog site http://blog.apastyle.org/ and Purdue University's Online Writing Lab (OWL) APA style site at http://owl.english.purdue.edu/owl/resource/560/02/.

Section G
Chicago referencing style

There are two formats within Chicago referencing style: Notes and Bibliography (NB), and Author-Date. The Chicago NB format is used in the humanities, see below. The Author-Date format is used in social sciences (see page 120).

Chicago Notes and Bibliography (NB) format

This format uses **footnotes** below your text and a **bibliography** at the end of your text.

Instead of naming authors in the text, which can be distracting for the reader, numbers are used to denote **citations**. These numbers in the text are linked to a full **reference** in **footnotes** or **endnotes** and in your **bibliography**. Word-processing software such as Microsoft Word can create this link between citation number and full reference.

Cited publications are numbered in the order in which they are first referred to in the text. They are usually identified by a **superscript number**, for example, 'Thomas corrected this error'.[1]

Conventions when using the Chicago NB referencing style

Footnotes or endnotes

- Check whether footnotes or endnotes are preferred for the work you are producing
- All notes end with a full stop.

Author names

- In the footnotes, author names should be forename followed by surname, for example Francis Wheen. In the bibliography, author names should be surname followed by forename, for example Wheen, Francis
- If there are up to three authors of a source, give their names in your references, in the order they are shown in the source. If there are four or more authors, give the name of the first author, followed by **et al**. in the footnotes, but list all authors in the Bibliography. The first author's name is given in the Bibliography as surname, first name, but other authors are written as first name surname.

Titles

- Italicise the titles of books, journals and websites. Titles of articles, chapters, unpublished sources such as PhDs, and web pages within a website are placed within double quotation marks.

Bibliography

- List works in alphabetical order by surname of the first author
- Names are given as surname, forename for the first author, but subsequent authors and editors are given as forename surname. For example: Williams, Edith, Jane Thompson and Claire Hopper
- Sources without an author are listed by title in the alphabetical list
- References in your bibliography end with a full stop
- As well as footnotes or endnotes, you should list all your sources, including those you have read but not cited, in the bibliography.

First citation and subsequent short citations

The first time you cite a source give full details in the footnote or endnote. Subsequent entries of the same source can be abbreviated to author's surname and the first few words of the title, plus a page number if you are citing a specific part of the text, giving you a **short citation**, for example:

Worsley, *Classical Architecture*, p. 25.

The sample text at the end of this section shows examples of a first citation and subsequent short citation of this book by Worsley.

Ibid.

- Ibid. (from Latin, *ibidem*) means 'in the same place'. If two (or more) consecutive references are from the same source, then the second (or others) is cited ibid. Capitalise ibid. if used at the beginning of a note, for example:
  1. Paulina Grainger, *Imagery in Prose*, London: Dale Press, 2009, pp. 133–81.
  2. Ibid., p. 155.
  3. Ibid., p. 170.

Capitalisation

- Capitalise the first letter of the first word of the title and subtitle and subsequent main words (but not articles such as the, of, and). Capitalise articles if they are the first words of a subtitle after a colon, for example *Cite Them Right: The Essential Referencing Guide*.

Dates

- For serials such as journals and newspapers dates should be written as month day, year.

Place of publication: publisher, year of publication

- All in round brackets in footnotes but not in bibliography.

Internet addresses (URLs) and Digital Object Identifiers (DOIs)

- The URL is given in full

- Place the accessed date before the URL
- DOIs should be used if they are available as these are a permanent locator, instead of URLs. If using a DOI you do not need to give the accessed date.

Page numbers

- Omit p. or pp. but give page numbers for references to information cited, paraphrasing or quotations taken from the original source
- In the footnote give the specific page number of information you have used in a source after the publication details. In the bibliography give the span of pages of the whole chapter or section you have used in an edited book before the publication details.

Formatting and punctuation

- Chicago referencing style has regulations for formatting your footnotes and references. The first line of footnotes should be indented by ½ inch (1.3cm) and subsequent lines are not indented. For the bibliography the first line of references is not indented, but the second and subsequent lines have a hanging indent of ½ inch (1.3cm)
- Chicago style has different punctuation for entries in your footnotes and in your bibliography. Use commas to separate elements of the reference in the footnote but use commas or full stops to separate the elements of the reference in the bibliography. In your footnote the place of publication, publisher and year are enclosed in round brackets, but are unenclosed in the bibliography entry. Editors are referred to as 'ed.' in the footnote but the phrase 'edited by' is used in the bibliography.

Example

Footnote

1. Jane Dickson, "Female Managers in Industry," in *Corporate Leadership*, ed. Javid Singh (Oxford: Oxford University Press, 2014), 49.

Bibliography

Dickson, Jane. "Female Managers in Industry." In *Corporate Leadership*, edited by Javid Singh, 48–56. Oxford: Oxford University Press, 2014.

How to reference common sources in footnotes and bibliography

G1 Books

Citation order:

- Author
- Title (in italics)
- Edition (only include the edition number if it is not the first edition)
- Place of publication: publisher, year of publication (all in round brackets in footnote but not in bibliography)
- Comma then page reference in footnote

Example

Footnote

1. Giles Worsley, *Classical Architecture in Britain: The Heroic Age* (London: Published for the Paul Mellon Centre for Studies in British Art by Yale University Press, 1995), 47.

Bibliography

Worsley, Giles. *Classical Architecture in Britain: The Heroic Age*. London: Published for the Paul Mellon Centre for Studies in British Art by Yale University Press, 1995.

G2 Ebooks

Cite ebooks in the same format as print books, but add details of the medium you used at the end of the reference. If you have read the book online give the DOI or URL and date accessed. If you have read the ebook on a personal device state the format, for example Kindle edition, Sony ebook, PDF. If you are unable to give page numbers for an ebook give the most accurate information that you can, such as chapter.

Citation order in the footnote:

- Author/editor
- Title (in italics)
- Edition (only include the edition number if it is not the first edition)
- Place of publication: publisher, year of publication (all in round brackets in footnote but not in bibliography)
- doi

OR

- Comma then accessed month day, year
- URL of collection
- Page reference

Citation order in the bibliography:

- Author/editor
- Title (in italics)
- Edition (only include the edition number if it is not the first edition)
- Place of publication: publisher, year of publication
- doi

OR

- Accessed month day, year
- URL of collection

> **Example**
>
> **Footnote**
>
> 1. Robert Adam, *Ruins of the Palace of the Emperor Diocletian at Spalatro in Dalmatia* (London: Printed for the author, 1764), accessed December 21, 2015. http://galenet.galegroup.com/servlet/ECCO, plate 14.
>
> **Bibliography**
>
> Adam, Robert. *Ruins of the Palace of the Emperor Diocletian at Spalatro in Dalmatia.* London: Printed for the author, 1764. Accessed December 21, 2015. http://galenet.galegroup.com/servlet/ECCO.

G3   Chapters of edited books

Citation order:

- Author of the chapter
- Title of chapter (in double quotation marks)
- in (when used in footnote, In when used in Bibliography)
- Title of book (in italics)
- ed. or edited by
- Name of editor of book (first name surname)
- Page span of chapter or section (only in bibliography)
- Place of publication: publisher, year of publication (all in round brackets in footnote but not in bibliography)
- Comma then page reference in footnote

> **Example**
>
> **Footnote**
>
> 1. Alexandrina Buchanan, "Interpretations of Medieval Architecture," in *Gothic Architecture and Its Meanings 1550–1830*, ed. Michael Hall (Reading: Spire Books, 2002), 32.
>
> **Bibliography**
>
> Buchanan, Alexandrina. "Interpretations of Medieval Architecture." In *Gothic Architecture and Its Meanings 1550–1830*, edited by Michael Hall, 27–52. Reading: Spire Books, 2002.

G4   Plays

Citation order:

- Author
- Title (in italics)
- Edited by forename/surname
- Place of publication: publisher, year
- Reference to cited Act. Scene. Line number, or page number

> **Example**
>
> **Footnote**
>
> 1. William Shakespeare, *Hamlet*, ed. by T.J.B. Spencer (London: Penguin, 1980), I.2.177.
>
> **Bibliography**
>
> Shakespeare, William. *Hamlet*, Edited by T.J.B. Spencer. London: Penguin, 1980.

G5   Journal articles

Citation order:

- Author
- Title of article (in double quotation marks)
- Title of journal (in italics)
- Volume number, issue number
- Year of publication (in round brackets)

- Colon then page reference in footnote or page span in bibliography

---

Example

Footnote

1. Peter Leach, "James Paine's Design for the South Front of Kedleston Hall: Dating and Sources," *Architectural History* 40 (1997): 160.

Bibliography

Leach, Peter. "James Paine's Design for the South Front of Kedleston Hall: Dating and Sources." *Architectural History* 40 (1997):159–70.

G6 Ejournal articles

Citation order:

- Author
- Title of article (in double quotation marks)
- Title of journal (in italics)
- Volume number, issue number
- Year of publication (in round brackets)
- Colon then page reference in footnote or page span in bibliography
- doi

OR

- Comma then accessed month day, year (in footnote) OR full stop Accessed month day, year (in bibliography)
- URL

NB *Chicago Manual of Style* states that access dates are not required for stable, published sources (for example JSTOR) but it recognises that some disciplines and many universities require access dates to be included in references. The following examples show references with and without accessed dates.

Example: footnote with URL and accessed date

1. S. Lang, "The Principles of the Gothic Revival in England," *Journal of the Society of Architectural Historians* 25, no. 4 (1966): 244, accessed December 21, 2015, http://www.jstor.org/stable/988353.

Example: footnote with doi

2. Edwina Thomas Washington, "An Overview of Cyberbullying in Higher Education," *Adult Learning* 26 (2015): 21–27, doi: 10.1177/1045159514558412.

Bibliography

Lang, S. "The Principles of the Gothic Revival in England." *Journal of the Society of Architectural Historians* 25, no. 4 (1966): 240–67. Accessed December 21, 2015. http://www.jstor.org/stable/988353.

Washington, Edwina Thomas. "An Overview of Cyberbullying in Higher Education." *Adult Learning* 26 (2015): 21–27. doi: 10.1177/1045159514558412.

G7 Newspaper and magazine articles

Citation order:

- Author
- Title of article (in double quotation marks)
- Title of newspaper (in italics)
- Date
- Section (if applicable)

NB Omit articles from newspaper titles, for example write *Times*, not *The Times*. Add a location if this helps to identify it, for example *Journal* (Newcastle upon Tyne).

G8   Theses and dissertations

Citation order:

- Author
- Title of thesis (in double quotation marks)
- Degree level, university, year
- Page reference in footnote

Note that Chicago style follows the American terminology for Master's thesis and PhD dissertation (rather than Master's dissertation and PhD thesis as in the UK).

If you have read the thesis or dissertation online, add the name of the database and accession number, or the URL and accessed date.

G9   Conference papers

Citation order:

- Author
- Title of paper (in double quotation marks)
- Paper presented at
- Name of conference, location and date.

G10   Book reviews

Citation order:

- Author of review
- Title of review article (in double quotation marks)
- Review of
- Title of work being reviewed (in italics)

- By
- Name of author of work being reviewed
- Title of publication where review published (in italics)
- Date
- Section
- Page number or URL

> **Example**
>
> **Footnote**
>
> 1. Willy Maley, "Where No Man Has Gone Before," review of *Samuel Johnson and the Journey into Words*, by Lynda Mugglestone, *Times Higher Education*, September 24, 2015, Books, 42.
>
> **Bibliography**
>
> Maley, Willy. "Where No Man Has Gone Before." Review of *Samuel Johnson and the Journey into Words*, by Lynda Mugglestone. *Times Higher Education*. September 24, 2015. Books, 42.

G11　Official publications

Citation order:
- Name of country
- Name of committee, department or Royal Commission
- Title (in italics)
- Volume details and command number if available
- Place of publication: publisher, year
- Accessed date and URL (if online)

> **Example**
>
> **Footnote**
>
> 1. United Kingdom, Department for Business Innovation & Skills, *Regulations Implementing the National Minimum Wage – a Report on the Apprentice Rate*, Cm 9061 (London: The Stationery Office, 2015) accessed: September 17, 2015, https://www.gov.uk/government/publications/national-minimum-wage-report-on-the-2015-apprentice-rate.
>
> 2. United Kingdom, Secretary of State for Prices and Consumer Protection, *Review of Restrictive Trade Practices Policy*, Cmnd 7512 (London: HMSO, 1979).
>
> **Bibliography**
>
> United Kingdom. Department for Business Innovation & Skills. *Regulations Implementing the National Minimum Wage – a Report on the Apprentice Rate*. Cm 9061. London: The Stationery Office, 2015. Accessed: September 17, 2015. https://www.gov.uk/government/publications/national-minimum-wage-report-on-the-2015-apprentice-rate.
>
> United Kingdom. Secretary of State for Prices and Consumer Protection. *Review of Restrictive Trade Practices Policy*. Cmnd 7512. London: HMSO, 1979.

G12　Music scores

Citation order:
- Composer
- Title of work (in italics)
- Place of publication: publisher, year

G13 Organisation or personal internet sites

If the details of the website can be given in your text you do not need to add a footnote and bibliography entry, for example: "The text was published on the Auden Society website on August 4, 2015." If you are providing footnote and bibliography entries, use:

Citation order in footnote:

- Title of internet site (in double quotation marks)
- Author/organisation
- accessed date OR date last modified
- URL

Citation order in bibliography:

- Author/organisation
- Title of internet site (in double quotation marks)
- accessed date OR date last modified
- URL

G14 Facebook

Citation order:

- Title
- accessed date
- URL

G15 Twitter

You can include the details of a tweet in a sentence. For example: "In her Twitter post of November 14, 2015, Jane March (@jmarch) stated, 'University entry grades rose by an average of four points in 2015.'" If you wish to give footnote and bibliography entries use:

Citation order:

- Author
- Twitter post
- Date and time
- URL

> **Example**
>
> **Footnote**
>
> 1. Jane March, Twitter post, November 14, 2015, 1.20 p.m., http://twitter.com/jmarch.
>
> **Bibliography**
>
> March, Jane. Twitter post. November 14, 2015, 1.20 p.m. http://twitter.com/jmarch.

G16 Emails

Email messages can be cited in your text rather than in a footnote or bibliography. For example: "In her email to the author on December 1, 2015 Amanda Hollis listed …" If you wish to cite an email, do so in a footnote:

> **Example**
>
> **Footnote**
>
> 1. Amanda Hollis, email message to the author, December 1, 2015.

G17 Manuscripts in archives

When citing archive sources in your footnote, begin with the item you are citing rather than the full collection. However, in your bibliography begin with the name of the collection. If you are citing only one item from a collection give full details in the bibliography, but if citing two or more you need provide only one reference to the collection in the bibliography.

Citation order:
- Place
- Name of archive
- Reference number
- Description of document

> **Example**
>
> **Footnote**
>
> 1. Howick Hall in 1926 showing fire damage, Photographs 20248/6-8, Sir Herbert Baker Collection, Royal Institute of British Architects Library, London.
>
> **Bibliography**
>
> Sir Herbert Baker Collection. Royal Institute of British Architects Library, London.

G18 Films

Citation order:
- Film title (in italics)
- Directed by First name Last name
- Year released;
- Place: distributor, year
- Format

> **Example**
>
> **Footnote**
>
> 1. *Brief Encounter*, directed by David Lean (1945; London: ITV Studios Home Entertainment, 2009), Blu-ray.
>
> **Bibliography**
>
> *Brief Encounter*. Directed by David Lean.1945. London: ITV Studios Home Entertainment, 2009. Blu-ray.

G19 Television or radio broadcasts

Citation order:
- Episode title (if applicable, in double quotation marks)
- Programme/series title (in italics)
- Name of broadcaster/channel
- month, day, year

Example

Footnote

1. "Scarlet Macaw," *Tweet of the Day*, BBC Radio 4, February 2, 2015.

Bibliography

"Scarlet Macaw." *Tweet of the Day*. BBC Radio 4, February 2, 2015.

G20 Art

Citation order:

- Artist
- Title of work (in italics)
- Date
- Medium
- Dimensions
- Location

Example

Footnote

1. John Martin, *The Bard*, 1817, oil on canvas 215cm × 157cm, Laing Art Gallery, Newcastle upon Tyne.

Bibliography

Martin, John. *The Bard*, 1817, oil on canvas 215cm × 157cm. Laing Art Gallery, Newcastle upon Tyne.

Sample text

This sample piece of text shows how various sources would be included as in-text citations:

Worsley's *Classical Architecture* highlighted the variety of styles that eighteenth-century architects employed in their buildings.[1] Rich patrons wanted designs in the latest fashion and among those to profit from this demand was Robert Adam, who published his studies of Roman buildings.[2] With this first-hand knowledge he designed many country houses and public buildings, and was even able to take over projects begun by other architects, as at Kedleston in Derbyshire.[3] His work was not always as revolutionary as he claimed,[4] but it certainly impressed clients and was copied by other architects including John Carr.[5] Although most patrons favoured classical styles, Horace Walpole suggested that the Gothic style was 'our architecture', the national style of England.[6] Later authors have suggested that Gothic style signified ancient lineage and the British Constitution.[7]

Sample footnotes

NB The first line of each footnote is indented by 1.3cm (½ inch). Text should be double-spaced.

1. Giles Worsley, *Classical Architecture in Britain: The Heroic Age* (London: Published for the Paul Mellon Centre for Studies in British Art by Yale University Press, 1995), 47.

2. Robert Adam, *Ruins of the Palace of the Emperor Diocletian at Spalatro in Dalmatia* (London: Printed for the author, 1764), accessed December 21, 2015. http://galenet.galegroup.com/servlet/ECCO.

3. Peter Leach, "James Paine's Design for the South Front of Kedleston Hall: Dating and Sources," *Architectural History* 40 (1997): 160.

4. Worsley, *Classical Architecture*, 265.

5. Brian Wragg, "The Life and Works of John Carr of York: Palladian Architect" (PhD diss., University of Sheffield, 1976).

6. Horace Walpole, cited in S. Lang, "The Principles of the Gothic Revival in England," *Journal of the Society of Architectural Historians* 25, no. 4 (1966): 244, accessed December 21, 2015, http://www.jstor.org/stable/988353.

7. Alexandrina Buchanan, "Interpretations of Medieval Architecture," in *Gothic Architecture and Its Meanings 1550–1830*, ed. Michael Hall (Reading: Spire Books, 2002): 27–52.

NB Footnote 4 is an example of a short citation, and footnote 6 is a secondary reference.

Sample bibliography

NB Sources listed in your bibliography should have a hanging indent of 1.3cm (½ inch) and text should be double-spaced.

Adam, Robert, *Ruins of the Palace of the Emperor Diocletian at Spalatro in Dalmatia* London: Printed for the author, 1764. Accessed December 21, 2015. http://galenet.galegroup.com/servlet/ECCO.

Buchanan, Alexandrina. "Interpretations of Medieval Architecture." In *Gothic Architecture and Its Meanings 1550–1830*, edited by Michael Hall, 27–52. Reading: Spire Books, 2002.

Lang, S., "The Principles of the Gothic Revival in England." *Journal of the Society of Architectural Historians* 25, no. 4 (1966): 240–67. Accessed December 21, 2015, http://www.jstor.org/stable/988353.

Leach, Peter. "James Paine's Design for the South Front of Kedleston Hall: Dating and Sources." *Architectural History* 40 (1997):159–70.

Worsley, Giles, *Classical Architecture in Britain: The Heroic Age* London: Published for the Paul Mellon Centre for Studies in British Art by Yale University Press, 1995.

Wragg, Brian. "The Life and Works of John Carr of York: Palladian Architect." PhD diss., University of Sheffield, 1976.

NB For more information on using the Chicago referencing style, see *Chicago manual of style* (2010) 16th edn. Chicago: University of Chicago Press; and *Chicago style citation quick guide* (2015) Available at: http://www.chicagomanualofstyle.org/tools_citationguide.html (Accessed: 25 September 2015).

Chicago Author-Date format

As with APA and Harvard styles, the Chicago Author-Date format uses in-text citations comprising the author's name and year of publication (and specific page reference if required).

Example of in-text citation

Washington (2015, 27) concurred with an earlier assessment (Dickson 2014) …

A reference list (rather than a bibliography) at the end of the work provides full bibliographical details for sources used. These sources are listed in alphabetical order by authors' names.

The major difference in the form of the references is the position of the year of publication. In the Notes and Bibliography format the year comes towards the end of the reference, but in Author-Date format it is moved to second place in the reference, after the author's name, or if this is unavailable, the title of the source.

Examples

Bibliography in NB format:

Dickson, Jane. "Female Managers in Industry." In Corporate Leadership, edited by Javid Singh, 48–56. Oxford: Oxford University Press, 2014.

Washington, Edwina Thomas. "An Overview of Cyberbullying in Higher Education." Adult Learning 26 (2015): 21–27. doi: 10.1177/1045159514558412.

Reference list in Author-Date format:

Dickson, Jane. 2014. "Female Managers in Industry." In Corporate Leadership, edited by Javid Singh, 48–56. Oxford: Oxford University Press.

Washington, Edwina Thomas. 2015. "An Overview of Cyberbullying in Higher Education." Adult Learning 26: 21–27. doi: 10.1177/1045159514558412.

Note how the date now comes after the author's name and that the date is also without round brackets in Author-Date format. Other details and punctuation in Author-Date format match the examples for Notes and Bibliography format.

Footnotes in Author-Date format

Unlike APA and Harvard, Chicago Author-Date format allows the use of footnotes to elaborate on something you have mentioned in the text. Footnotes are NOT used to give full bibliographic details, which are given in the reference list.

Example: in-text citation with footnote

Washington (2015, 27) concurred with an earlier assessment.[1]

Footnote

1. Dickson (2014, 50) had examined bullying in male-dominated occupations.

Section H
Modern Humanities Research Association (MHRA) referencing style

The MHRA referencing style is used in some arts and humanities publications.

Citing sources in your text

Instead of naming authors in the text, which can be distracting for the reader, numbers are used to denote **citations**. These numbers in the text are linked to a full **reference** in **footnotes** or **endnotes** and in your **bibliography**. Word-processing software such as Microsoft Word can create this link between citation number and full reference.

Cited publications are numbered in the order in which they are first referred to in the text. They are usually identified by a **superscript number**, for example 'Thomas corrected this error.[1]' Superscript numbers can be created in Microsoft Word by selecting 'References' from the Menu bar, then 'Insert Footnote'.

Conventions when using the MHRA referencing style

Footnotes and endnotes

- Check whether footnotes or endnotes are preferred for the work you are producing
- All footnotes or endnotes end with a full stop.

Author names

- Note that in the footnotes, author names should be forename followed by surname, for example Francis Wheen. In the bibliography, author names should be surname followed by forename, for example Wheen, Francis
- If there are up to three authors of a source, give their names in your bibliography, in the order they are shown in the source. If there are four or more authors, give the name of the first author, followed by 'and others'.

Bibliography

- List works in alphabetical order by surname of the first author
- Names are given as surname, forename for the first author, but subsequent authors and editors are given as forename, surname. For example: Williams, Edith, Jane Thompson and Claire Hopper
- Sources without an author are listed by title in the alphabetical list
- References in your bibliography do not end with a full stop
- Indent the second and subsequent lines of each reference in the bibliography but not in footnotes
- As well as footnotes or endnotes, you should list all your sources, including those you have read but not cited, in the bibliography.

First citation and subsequent short citations

- Note that the first time you cite a source, you should give full details in the footnote or endnote. Subsequent entries to the same source can be abbreviated to author's surname and the first few words of the title, plus a page number if you are citing a specific part of the text, giving you a short citation, for example:

Worsley, *Classical Architecture*, p. 25.

The sample text at the end of this section shows examples of a first citation and subsequent short citation of this book by Worsley.

- Note that the use of short citations, which are more precise, replaces **op. cit.** which was previously used.

Ibid.

- **Ibid.** (from Latin, *ibidem*) means 'in the same place'. If two (or more) consecutive references are from the same source, then the second (or others) is cited ibid. Capitalise ibid. if used at the beginning of a note, for example:
  1. Paulina Grainger, *Imagery in Prose* (London: Dale Press, 2009), pp. 133–81.
  2. Ibid., p. 155.
  3. Ibid., p. 170.

Capitalisation

- Capitalise the first letter of the first word, all nouns, verbs and adjectives. Also capitalise articles if they are the first words of a subtitle after a colon, for example *Cite Them Right: The Essential Referencing Guide*.

Internet addresses (URLs) and Digital Object Identifiers (DOIs)

- The internet address is given in full, but with < in front and > after the address, for example <http://news.bbc.co.uk> then [accessed date]
- DOIs should be used if they are available as these are a permanent locator. If using a DOI you do not need to give the accessed date.

Commas

- Use commas to separate the elements of the reference.

Page numbers

- Use p. or pp. for books but not for journal articles.

How to reference common sources in footnotes and bibliography

H1   Books

Citation order:

- Author/editor
- Title (in italics)
- Edition (only include the edition number if it is not the first edition)
- Place of publication: publisher, year of publication (all in round brackets)

> **Example**
>
> **Footnote**
>
> 1. Giles Worsley, *Classical Architecture in Britain: The Heroic Age* (London: Published for the Paul Mellon Centre for Studies in British Art by Yale University Press, 1995), p. 47.
>
> **Bibliography**
>
> Worsley, Giles, *Classical Architecture in Britain: The Heroic Age* (London: Published for the Paul Mellon Centre for Studies in British Art by Yale University Press, 1995)

H2   Ebooks

Citation order:

- Author/editor
- Title (in italics)
- Edition (only include the edition number if it is not the first edition)
- Place of publication: publisher, year of publication (all in round brackets)
- in
- Title of online collection (in italics)
- <URL of collection>
- [accessed date]

Example

Footnote

1. Robert Adam, *Ruins of the Palace of the Emperor Diocletian at Spalatro in Dalmatia* (London: Printed for the author, 1764), in *Eighteenth Century Collections Online* <http://galenet.galegroup.com/servlet/ECCO> [accessed 21 December 2015], plate 14.

Bibliography

Adam, Robert, *Ruins of the Palace of the Emperor Diocletian at Spalatro in Dalmatia* (London: Printed for the author, 1764), in *Eighteenth Century Collections Online* <http://galenet.galegroup.com/servlet/ECCO> [accessed 21 December 2015]

H3 Chapters/sections of edited books

Citation order:

- Author of the chapter/section
- Title of chapter/section (in single quotation marks)
- in
- Title of book (in italics)
- ed. by
- Name of editor of book
- Place of publication: publisher, year of publication (all in round brackets)
- Page numbers of chapter/section (preceded by pp.)

Note: footnote reference has (p.).

Example

Footnote

1. Alexandrina Buchanan, 'Interpretations of Medieval Architecture', in *Gothic Architecture and Its Meanings 1550–1830*, ed. by Michael Hall (Reading: Spire Books, 2002), pp. 27–52 (p. 47).

Bibliography

Buchanan, Alexandrina, 'Interpretations of Medieval Architecture', in *Gothic Architecture and Its Meanings 1550–1830*, ed. by Michael Hall (Reading: Spire Books, 2002), pp. 27–52

H4 Translated works

Citation order:

- Author of original work
- Title (in italics)
- Trans. by name of translator (forename surname)
- Place of publication: publisher, year of publication (all in round brackets)

Example

Footnote

1. Ignazio Silone, *Fontamara*, trans. by Gwenda David and Eric Mosbacher (London: Redwords, 1994).

Bibliography

Silone, Ignazio, *Fontamara*, trans. by Gwenda David and Eric Mosbacher (London: Redwords, 1994)

H5 Plays

Citation order:

- Author
- Title
- ed. by forename surname
- Place of publication: publisher, year (in round brackets)

- Reference to cited Act. Scene. Line number, or page number

Example

Footnote

1. William Shakespeare, *Hamlet*, ed. by T.J.B. Spencer (London: Penguin, 1980), I. 2. 177.

Bibliography

Shakespeare, William, *Hamlet*, ed. by T.J.B. Spencer (London: Penguin, 1980)

H6 Journal articles

Citation order:

- Author
- Title of article (in single quotation marks)
- Title of journal (in italics and capitalise first letter of each word in title, except for linking words such as and, of, the, for)
- Volume number. Issue number
- Year of publication (in round brackets)
- Page numbers of article (not preceded by pp.)

Note: footnote reference has (p.).

Example

Footnote

1. Peter Leach, 'James Paine's Design for the South Front of Kedleston Hall: Dating and Sources', *Architectural History*, 40 (1997), 159–70 (p. 160).

Bibliography

Leach, Peter, 'James Paine's Design for the South Front of Kedleston Hall: Dating and Sources', *Architectural History*, 40 (1997), 159–70

H7 Ejournal articles

Citation order:

- Author
- Title of article (in single quotation marks)
- Title of journal (in italics and capitalise first letter of each word in title, except for linking words such as and, of, the, for)
- Volume number. Issue number
- Year of publication (in round brackets)
- Page numbers of article
- <URL> or <DOI>
- [accessed date] if required

Examples

Footnote with URL and accessed date

1. S. Lang, 'The Principles of the Gothic Revival in England', *Journal of the Society of Architectural Historians*, 25.4 (1966), 240–67 (p. 244) <http://www.jstor.org/stable/988353> [accessed 21 December 2015].

Footnote with DOI

1. Edwina Thomas Washington, 'An Overview of Cyberbullying in Higher Education', *Adult Learning*, 26 (2015), 21–27 (p. 26) DOI: 10.1177/1045159514558412.

Bibliography

Lang, S., 'The Principles of the Gothic Revival in England', *Journal of the Society of Architectural Historians*, 25.4 (1966), 240–67 <http://www.jstor.org/stable/988353> [accessed 21 December 2015]

Washington, Edwina Thomas, 'An Overview of Cyberbullying in Higher Education', *Adult Learning*, 26 (2015), 21–27 DOI: 10.1177/1045159514558412

H8 Newspaper and magazine articles

Citation order:

- Author
- Title of article (in single quotation marks)
- Title of newspaper (in italics and capitalise first letter of each word in title, except for linking words such as and, of, the, for)
- Date
- Section (if applicable)
- Page number, preceded by p.

> **Example**
>
> **Footnote**
>
> 1. Dan Hyde, 'Parents Funding Adult Offspring's Holidays', *Daily Telegraph*, 14 September 2015, p. 2.
>
> **Bibliography**
>
> Hyde, Dan, 'Parents Funding Adult Offspring's Holidays', *Daily Telegraph*, 14 September 2015, p. 2

H9 Theses and dissertations

Citation order:

- Author
- Title of thesis (in single quotation marks)
- Degree level, University, year (in round brackets)

> **Example**
>
> **Footnote**
>
> 1. Adrian Green, 'Houses and Households in County Durham and Newcastle c.1570–1730' (unpublished doctoral thesis, Durham University, 2000).
>
> **Bibliography**
>
> Green, Adrian, 'Houses and Households in County Durham and Newcastle c.1570–1730' (unpublished doctoral thesis, Durham University, 2000)

H10 Papers in published proceedings of a conference

Citation order:

- Author
- Title of paper (in single quotation marks)
- Title of conference proceedings publication (in italics)
- Editor
- (Place of publication: publisher, year)
- Page numbers

Example

Footnote

1. Mary Stephens, 'Wordsworth's Inspiration', *Proceedings of the Tenth Conference in Romance Studies, 18 May 2014*, ed. by Hilary Jones (Derby: University of Derby Press, 2014), pp. 27–39.

Bibliography

Stephens, Mary, 'Wordsworth's Inspiration', *Proceedings of the Tenth Conference in Romance Studies, 18 May 2014*, ed. by Hilary Jones (Derby: University of Derby Press, 2014), pp. 27–39

H11 Organisation or personal internet sites

Citation order:

- Author
- Title of internet site (in italics)
- Year that the site was published/last updated (in round brackets)
- <URL>
- [accessed date]

Example

Footnote

1. Salvatore Ciro Nappo, *Pompeii: Its Discovery and Preservation* (2012) <http://www.bbc.co.uk/history/ancient/romans/pompeii_rediscovery_01.shtml> [accessed 21 December 2015].

Bibliography

Nappo, Salvatore Ciro, *Pompeii: Its Discovery and Preservation* (2012) <http://www.bbc.co.uk/history/ancient/romans/pompeii_rediscovery_01.shtml> [accessed 21 December 2015]

For **web pages** where no author can be identified, you should use the web page's title. If there is no title either, use the URL.

Example

Footnote

1. *Palladio's Italian Villas* (2005) <http://www.boglewood.com/palladio/> [accessed 21 December 2015].

For the bibliography use the same format but omit the final full stop and indent the second and subsequent lines.

H12 Facebook

Give the full text of the Facebook post in your footnote and bibliography.

Citation order:

- Author
- Title of post (in single quotation marks)
- Medium (in square brackets)
- <URL>
- Date
- [accessed date]

H13   Twitter

The full text of tweets should be given, either in your text or in a footnote, retaining hashtags # and @handles.

Citation order:
- Author
- Title of post (in single quotation marks)
- Medium (in square brackets)
- hashtags # and @handle, date (in round brackets)

Example

`In-text`

Chris Cook tweeted that 'Theresa May says unis should "develop sustainable funding models that are not so dependent on international students"' (@xtophercook, 16 July 2015).[1]

`Footnote`

1. Chris Cook, 'Theresa May says unis should "develop sustainable funding models that are not so dependent on international students."' [Twitter post] (@xtophercook, 16 July 2015).

`Bibliography`

Cook, Chris, 'Theresa May says unis should "develop sustainable funding models that are not so dependent on international students."' [Twitter post] (@xtophercook, 16 July 2015)

H14   Emails

Citation order:
- Author
- Title of message (in single quotation marks)
- Email to recipient, date (in round brackets)

Example

`Footnote`

1. Maria Guevara, 'New Spanish Publications' (Email to Carlos Pererra, 16 July 2015).

`Bibliography`

Guevara, Maria, 'New Spanish Publications' (Email to Carlos Pererra, 16 July 2015)

H15   Manuscripts in archives

Citation order:
- Place
- Name of archive
- Reference number
- Description of document

Example

`Footnote`

1. London, The National Archives, Public Record Office, PROB 3/42/93 Inventory of Elizabeth Bennett of Deptford, 10 November 1743.

For the bibliography use the same format but omit the final full stop and indent the second and subsequent lines.

H16   Films

Citation order:
- Film title (in italics)
- dir. by forename surname
- Distributor, year (in round brackets)
- [on DVD]

Example

Footnote

1. *Brief Encounter*, dir. by David Lean (Eagle-Lion Distributors Ltd, 1945) [on DVD].

For the bibliography use the same format but omit the final full stop and indent the second and subsequent lines.

H17 Television or radio broadcasts

Citation order:

- Episode title (if applicable, in single quotation marks)
- Broadcast/programme/series title (in italics)
- Channel name
- Day month year
- Time of broadcast

Example

Footnote

1. 'Scarlet Macaw', *Tweet of the Day*, BBC Radio 4, 2 February 2015, 05.58.

For the bibliography use the same format but omit the final full stop and indent the second and subsequent lines.

H18 Sound recordings

Citation order:

- Composer
- Title (in italics)
- Artist, orchestra or conductor (as relevant)
- Recording company, CD reference, date (in round brackets)
- [on CD]

Example

Footnote

1. Gustav Mahler, *Symphony no. 10*, BBC National Orchestra of Wales, cond. by Mark Wigglesworth (BBC, MM124, 1994) [on CD].

Bibliography

Mahler, Gustav, *Symphony no. 10*, BBC National Orchestra of Wales, conducted by Mark Wigglesworth (BBC, MM124, 1994) [on CD]

H19 Music scores

Citation order:

- Composer
- Title of work (in italics)
- Place of publication: publisher, year (in round brackets)

Example

Footnote

1. Wolfgang A. Mozart, *Don Giovanni: Overture to the Opera*, K 527 (New York: Dover, 1964).

Bibliography

Mozart, Wolfgang A., *Don Giovanni: Overture to the Opera*, K 527 (New York: Dover, 1964)

H20 Art

Citation order:

- Artist
- Title of work (in italics)
- Date
- Medium
- Location

Sample text

This sample piece of text shows how various sources would be included as in-text citations:

Worsley's *Classical Architecture* highlighted the variety of styles that eighteenth-century architects employed in their buildings.[1] Initially British architects relied upon the designs of Andrea Palladio, a sixteenth-century Italian architect, who was believed to have studied ancient Roman buildings.[2] As the century progressed, however, more authentic Roman examples were studied, particularly after the discovery of Pompeii.[3] Rich patrons wanted designs in the latest fashion and among those to profit from this demand was Robert Adam, who published his studies of Roman architecture.[4] With this first-hand knowledge he designed many country houses and public buildings.[5] His work was not always as revolutionary as he claimed,[6] but it impressed clients. Adam was even able to take over projects begun by other architects, as at Kedleston in Derbyshire.[7]

Although most patrons favoured classical styles, Horace Walpole suggested that the Gothic style was 'our architecture', the national style of England.[8] Later authors have suggested that Gothic style signified ancient lineage and the British Constitution.[9]

Sample footnotes

1. Giles Worsley, *Classical Architecture in Britain: The Heroic Age* (London: Published for the Paul Mellon Centre for Studies in British Art by Yale University Press, 1995).

2. *Palladio's Italian Villas* (2005) <http://www.boglewood.com/palladio/> [accessed 21 December 2015].

3. Salvatore Ciro Nappo, *Pompeii: Its Discovery and Preservation* (2012) <http://www.bbc.co.uk/history/ancient/romans/pompeii_rediscovery_01.shtml> [accessed 21 December 2015].

4. Robert Adam, *Ruins of the Palace of the Emperor Diocletian at Spalatro in Dalmatia* (London: Printed for the author, 1764), in *Eighteenth Century Collections Online* <http://galenet.galegroup.com/servlet/ECCO> [accessed 21 December 2015].

5. *Treasures of Britain and Treasures of Ireland* (London: Reader's Digest Association Ltd, 1990).

6. Worsley, *Classical Architecture*, p. 265.

7. Peter Leach, 'James Paine's Design for the South Front of Kedleston Hall: Dating and Sources', *Architectural History,* 40 (1997),159–70.

8. Horace Walpole, cited in S. Lang, 'The Principles of the Gothic Revival in England', *Journal of the Society of Architectural Historians*, 25.4 (1966), 240–67 <http://www.jstor.org/stable/988353> [accessed 21 December 2015].

9. Alexandrina Buchanan, 'Interpretations of Medieval Architecture', in *Gothic Architecture and Its Meanings 1550–1830*, ed. by Michael Hall (Reading: Spire Books, 2002), pp. 27–52.

NB Footnote 6 is an example of a short citation, and footnote 8 is a secondary reference.

Sample bibliography

Adam, Robert, *Ruins of the Palace of the Emperor Diocletian at Spalatro in Dalmatia* (London: Printed for the author, 1764), in *Eighteenth Century Collections Online* <http://galenet.galegroup.com/servlet/ECCO> [accessed 21 December 2015]

Buchanan, Alexandrina, 'Interpretations of Medieval Architecture', in *Gothic Architecture and Its Meanings 1550–1830*, ed. by Michael Hall (Reading: Spire Books, 2002), pp. 27–52

Lang, S., 'The Principles of the Gothic Revival in England', *Journal of the Society of Architectural Historians*, 25.4 (1966), 240–67 <http://www.jstor.org/stable/988353> [accessed 21 December 2015]

Leach, Peter, 'James Paine's Design for the South Front of Kedleston Hall: Dating and Sources', *Architectural History*, 40 (1997), 159–70

Nappo, Salvatore Ciro, *Pompeii: Its Discovery and Preservation* (2012) <http://www.bbc.co.uk/history/ancient/romans/pompeii_rediscovery_01.shtml> [accessed 21 December 2015]

Palladio's Italian Villas (2005) <http://www.boglewood.com/palladio/> [accessed 21 December 2015]

Treasures of Britain and Treasures of Ireland (London: Reader's Digest Association Ltd, 1990)

Worsley, Giles, *Classical Architecture in Britain: The Heroic Age* (London: Published for the Paul Mellon Centre for Studies in British Art by Yale University Press, 1995)

NB For more information on using the MHRA referencing style, see MHRA (2013) *MHRA style guide*. 3rd edn. London: Modern Humanities Research Association. Available at: http://www.mhra.org.uk/Publications/Books/StyleGuide/download.shtml (Accessed: 26 September 2015).

Section I
Modern Language Association (MLA) referencing style

The MLA referencing style is often used in humanities subjects, including languages and literature. Emphasis is placed on the author's name (or if not available, the title of the source). The authors' full names, as written on the title pages, should be used. Sources are listed in alphabetical order in a **list of Works Cited** at the end of your work. Sources that are not cited in your text can be included in **footnotes** or **endnotes**. **In-text citations** use the author's name and if possible a page number within the source. To find the full details of the source being cited, the reader must refer to the list of Works Cited.

Conventions when using the MLA referencing style

Author's name

- For in-text citations and footnotes, give the author's name as forename(s) or initials followed by surname, for example Peter Leach. For the list of Works Cited, give surname, then forename(s) or initials, for example Leach, Peter

- If you have two authors with the same surname, use their forename initials in your in-text citations and list of Works Cited to distinguish them, for example A. Jones and C. Jones

- For two or three authors of a single work separate the authors' names with a comma and use 'and' before the last named. Note that in the list of Works Cited the first author is given as surname then forename but subsequent authors are given as forename then surname. For example, an in-text citation to Jones, Willis and Singh, and in the list of Works Cited a reference to Jones, Anne, Joan Willis and Avjeet Singh

- For four or more authors of a single work, you may either list all authors, or MLA permits the use of **et al**. after the first author. Note that et al. is not italicised. For example, 'Chan et al. (46) noted …'

- If you are citing more than one publication by the same author, include a short version of the title of each work in the in-text citation, for example 'Thornber's *Labour Pains* continued themes from her conference paper ("Political spin") …'. In the list of Works Cited, give the author's name for the first entry only and for subsequent references use three hyphens and a full stop ---. to replace the author's name.

Titles

- The titles of sources are italicised or placed in double quotation marks ""

- Capitalise the first word, all nouns, verbs and adjectives. Capitalise articles if they are the first words of a subtitle after a colon, for example *Cite Them Right: The Essential Referencing Guide*

- Non-English titles: give the title in the original language (unless you are using a translation) but you may include a short translated title after the original in square brackets, for example *I Quattro Libri Dell'Archittetura [The Four Books of Architecture]*.

Page numbers

- Do not use p. or pp. Page numbers of chapters and articles are elided, for example 127–45.

Date

- Give the year in the reference in the list of Works Cited
- If there is no date use n.d.

Abbreviations

MLA uses abbreviations in the list of Works Cited for time periods, organisation names, countries, counties and US states. A full list of abbreviations is given in chapter 7 of the 7th edition of the *MLA Handbook for Writers of Research Papers* (7th edn) and this should be consulted for specific examples, as there are many exceptions.

- When abbreviations are made up of capital letters it is common to omit full stops and spaces after the initial, for example AD and DVD, but when giving authors' initials use full stops and spaces, for example J. R. Hartley. When abbreviations are in lower-case letters, use full stops and no spaces between the letters, for example i.e. and e.g. However, there are exceptions to this, including mph. If the abbreviated word ends in a lower case letter add a full stop after the last letter, for example, academy is abbreviated to acad.
- Spell out names of months and days in your text but abbreviate them in the list of Works Cited, for example: Jan., Feb., Mar., Apr., May, June, July, Aug., Sept., Oct., Nov. and Dec. and Mon., Tues., Wed., Thurs., Fri., Sat. and Sun.
- When writing organisation and publisher names write out Incorporated, Company, Corporation, Limited in your text but omit Inc., Co., Corp., Ltd. from references in the list of Works Cited
- If the publisher name has several names, list only the first one in your list of Works Cited, for example McGraw Hill Education would be written as McGraw. If the publisher name is a person's name this is abbreviated to surname only, for example

John Wiley & Sons would be written as Wiley

- If a publisher name contains the word Press, for example Summerhill Press, this is abbreviated to Summerhill in the list of Works Cited. However, if the publisher is a university the word University is replaced by a U and Press is replaced by the initial P in the list of Works Cited; neither have full stops after the initial. For example write out Oxford University Press in your text but abbreviate to Oxford UP in the list of Works Cited.

Medium

At the end of the reference include the medium in which you have used the source, for example Print for print publications. The 7th edition of the *MLA Handbook for Writers of Research Papers*. New York: Modern Language Association of America, 2009, replaced the **URL** of a website at the end of the reference with the word Web to denote the medium of publication. This assumes that most readers will be able to locate an online source using a search engine. You should only include the URL in angle brackets, for example <URL> after the date of access if you think that a reader will be unable to locate a source using a search engine (see Section I14).

Footnotes or endnotes

- You can use footnotes or endnotes in the MLA referencing style to bring in additional information. Use a **superscript number** for the footnote.

List of Works Cited

- All sources referenced in your work should be listed in Works Cited at the end of your text. Sources should be listed alphabetically by author. Second and subsequent lines of the reference should be indented by ½ inch (1.3cm).

How to cite common sources in your text

You can phrase your text to note the author's view.

> **Example**
>
> Francis Wheen compared Thatcher's dislike of trade unions to that of Victorian mill-owners (23).

Or you can cite the author and page number after the section of their work you have referred to.

> **Example**
>
> Margaret Thatcher had a 'hostility to organised labour that would have won the respect of any grim-visaged Victorian mill-owner' (Wheen 23).

Note that there is no comma between the author and the page number and that there is no p. before the page number. If there is no author, use the title of the source and the page number.

> **Example**
>
> The Percy tomb has been described as 'one of the masterpieces of medieval European art' (*Treasures of Britain* 84).

How to reference common sources in the list of Works Cited

I1   Books

Citation order:

- Author/editor (surname, forename)
- Title (in italics)
- Edition (only include the edition number if it is not the first edition)
- Place of publication: publisher
- Year of publication
- Medium

> **Example**
>
> Works Cited
>
> Worsley, Giles. *Classical Architecture in Britain: The Heroic Age*. New Haven: Yale UP, 1995. Print.

I2   Ebooks

Use this format for books available through your institution's library or through an online provider such as *Google Books* or *Archive.org*.

Citation order:

- Author/editor (surname, forename)
- Title (in italics)
- Edition (only include the edition number if it is not the first edition)
- Place of publication: publisher
- Year of publication
- Name of database or collection (in italics)
- Web
- Date of access

> **Example**
>
> Works Cited
>
> Hornstein, Shelley. *Losing Site: Architecture, Memory and Place*. Farnham: Ashgate, 2011. *MyiLibrary*. Web. 21 August 2015.

If you are viewing the book on a personal device, use the file type as the medium.

Citation order:

- Author/editor (surname, forename)
- Title (in italics)
- Edition (only include the edition number if it is not the first edition)
- Place of publication: publisher
- Year of publication
- Medium

> **Example**
>
> `Works Cited`
>
> Pratchett, Terry. *The Shepherd's Crown*. London: Doubleday, 2015. Kindle file.

Although ebook readers may have numbering systems to indicate your position in the book such as percentage read, MLA advises not to use these as they will differ between mediums. Only use stable numbering systems such as chapters, abbreviated to ch., or page numbers if it is a PDF file.

I3 Chapters/sections of edited books

Citation order:

- Author of the chapter/section (surname, forename)
- Title of chapter/section (in double quotation marks)
- Title of book (in italics)
- Ed. and name of editor of book
- Place of publication: publisher
- Year of publication
- Page numbers of chapter/section
- Medium

> **Example**
>
> `Works Cited`
>
> Buchanan, Alexandrina. "Interpretations of Medieval Architecture." *Gothic Architecture and Its Meanings 1550–1830*. Ed. Michael Hall. Reading: Spire, 2002, 27–52. Print.

I4 Anthologies

Citation order:

- Author/editor (surname, forename)
- ed. or eds. (if editor)
- Title (in italics)

- Edition (only include the edition number if it is not the first edition)
- Place of publication: publisher
- Year of publication
- Medium of publication

> **Example**
>
> `Works Cited`
>
> Keane, Donald, ed. *Anthology of Japanese Literature*. New York: Grove, 1955. Print.

I5 Translated works

Citation order:

- Author/editor (surname, forename)
- Title (in italics)
- Trans.
- Name of translator (forename, surname)
- Place of publication: publisher
- Year of publication
- Medium of publication

> **Example**
>
> `Works Cited`
>
> Silone, Ignazio. *Fontamara*. Trans. Gwenda David and Eric Mosbacher. London: Redwords, 1994. Print.

I6 Book reviews

Citation order:

- Reviewer (surname, forename)
- Rev. of
- Title of book being reviewed (in italics)
- by
- Author of book being reviewed (forename, surname).
- Publication title (in italics)
- Date:
- Page numbers
- Medium of publication

Example

`Works Cited`

Ward, Paul. Rev. of *The English and Their History*, by Robert Tombs. *History Today* Mar. 2015: 60–61. Print.

I7 Journal articles

Citation order:

- Author (surname, forename)
- Title of article (in double quotation marks)
- Title of journal (in italics)
- Volume number. Issue number
- Year of publication (in round brackets) followed by colon
- Page numbers of journal article
- Medium

Example

`Works Cited`

Leach, Peter. "James Paine's Design for the South Front of Kedleston Hall: Dating and Sources." *Architectural History* 40 (1997): 159–70. Print.

I8 Ejournal articles

Citation order:

- Author (surname, forename or initial)
- Title of article (in double quotation marks)
- Title of journal (in italics)
- Volume number. Issue number
- Year (in round brackets) followed by colon
- Page numbers of article
- Name of collection (in italics)
- Web
- Date of access

Example

`Works Cited`

Lang, S. "The Principles of the Gothic Revival in England." *Journal of the Society of Architectural Historians* 25.4 (1966): 240–67. *JSTOR*. Web. 21 Aug. 2012.

I9 Magazine articles

Citation order:

- Author (surname, forename)
- Title of article (in double quotation marks)
- Title of magazine (in italics)
- Volume number and issue number
- Year of publication followed by colon
- Page numbers of printed magazine article
- Medium of publication
- Add date accessed if online

Example: print article

`Works Cited`

Bletcher, Katherine. "Matters of the Heart." *Heart Matters* Aug./Sept. 2012: 9–11. Print.

Example: online article

`Works Cited`

Bletcher, Katherine. "Matters of the Heart." *Heart Matters* Aug./Sept. 2012. Web. 22 Aug. 2015.

Note that the web version of the article does not have page numbers so these are omitted.

I10 Newspaper articles

Citation order:

- Author (surname, forename)
- Title of article (in double quotation marks)
- Title of newspaper (in italics) and omit '*The*'

- Volume number and issue number
- Year of publication followed by colon
- Page numbers of newspaper article
- Title of database in italics (if applicable)
- Medium of publication
- Date retrieved from database (if applicable)

Example: print article

Works Cited

Mansell, William and Bloom, Anne. "£10,000 Carrot to Tempt Physics Experts." *Guardian* 20 Jun. 2012: 5. Print.

Example: online article from a database

Works Cited

Mansell, William and Bloom, Anne. "£10,000 Carrot to Tempt Physics Experts." *Guardian* 20 Jun. 2012: 5. *Factiva*. Web. 19 Aug. 2015.

I11 Theses and dissertations

Citation order:

- Author (surname, forename)
- Title of thesis or dissertation (in double quotation marks)
- Level of qualification
- Awarding institution
- Year of award
- Repository name (if online, in italics)
- Medium
- Date if accessed online

Examples

Works Cited

Goldoni, Marcia. "The Development of Baroque Music in Italy." Diss. Nottingham U, 2011. Print.

Lebraun, Celine. "Imagery and Walt Whitman." Diss. Chicago U, 2008. *ProQuest Digital Dissertations*. Web. 9 Sept. 2015.

I12 Papers in published proceedings of a conference

Citation order:

- Author (surname, forename)
- Title of article (in double quotation marks)
- Title of conference proceedings (in italics)
- Date of conference
- Ed. and name of editor of conference proceedings
- Place of publication: publisher
- Year of publication
- Page numbers of chapter/section
- Medium
- Date if accessed online

Examples

Works Cited

Stephens, Mary. "Wordsworth's Inspiration." *Proceedings of the Tenth Conference in Romance Studies, 18 May 2014*. Ed. Hilary Jones. Derby: U of Derby P, 2014. 27–39. Print.

Worsley, Giles. "Adam as a Palladian." *Adam in Context: Papers Given at the Georgian Group Symposium 1992*. Ed. Giles Worsley. London: Georgian Group, 1993. 6–13. Print.

Example: online conference paper

`Works Cited`

Pettinger, Alasdair. "Frederick Douglass, Scotland and the South." *2003 Symbiosis Conference: 'Across the Great Divide' 14 December 2003*. Web. 22 Sept. 2015.

I13   Research reports

Research and technical reports may be produced by government, academics, business and industry in print and electronic formats.

Citation order:

- Country (if required)
- Author or department or organisation
- Title (in italics)
- Place of publication: publisher
- Year of publication
- Medium
- Date if accessed online

Examples

`Works Cited`

Great Britain. Department of Health. *Health Inequalities: Progress and Next Steps*. London: TSO, 2008. Print.

United Nations Development Programme. *Human Development Report 2014: Sustaining Human Progress: Reducing Vulnerabilities and Building Resilience*. 2014. Web. 9 Feb. 2016.

I14   Organisation or personal internet sites

Citation order:

- Author (surname, forename)
- Title of internet site (in italics)
- Year that the site was published/last updated
- Web
- Date of access
- <URL> (if it needs to be included)

Example

`Works Cited`

Nappo, Salvatore. *Pompeii: Its Discovery and Preservation,* 2012. Web. 21 Nov. 2015.

Below are examples of web pages where pieces of information are not available. Remember, you should always question the validity of sources where crucial elements are missing in order to establish the academic credibility of the source.

I14.1   Web pages with no authors

Citation order:

- Title of internet site (in italics)
- Year or n.d.
- Web
- Date of access
- <URL> (if it needs to be included)

Example, including URL

`Works Cited`

Palladio's Italian Villas. 2005. Web. 21 Sept. 2015. <http://www.boglewood.com/palladio/>.

I14.2   Web pages with no date

Citation order:

- Author (surname, forename)
- Title of internet site (in italics)
- n.d.
- Web
- Date of access
- <URL> (if it needs to be included)

> **Example**
>
> `Works Cited`
>
> English Heritage. *Georgians: Architecture*.
>   n.d. Web. 9 July. 2015.

I14.3   Web pages with no authors or titles

If a web page has no author or title and you have only the URL for your reference, you should question whether or not it is suitable for academic work.

Citation order:

- Year or n.d.
- Web
- Date of access
- <URL> (if it needs to be included)

> **Example**
>
> `Works Cited`
>
> n.d. Web. 29 Dec. 2015. <www.
>   dodgysite.com>.

I15   Blogs

Citation order:

- Author (surname, forename)
- Title of article (in double quotation marks)
- Title of blog (in italics)
- Publisher
- Date of post
- Web
- Date accessed

> **Example**
>
> `Works Cited`
>
> Ahmed, Kamal. "Business and Politicians
>   – Putting the Boots in". *BBC Business
>   Blog*. British Broadcasting Corporation
>   2 Feb. 2015. Web. 11 Feb. 2015.

I16   Facebook

Citation order:

- Author (surname, forename)
- Title of post (in double quotation marks)
- Date posted
- Facebook
- Web
- Date accessed

> **Example**
>
> `Works Cited`
>
> Jones, Mark. "Palace Green Library
>   Exhibitions." 9 July 2015. Facebook.
>   Web. 12 July. 2015.

I17   Twitter

Citation order:

- User's name (surname, forename – if known)
- Twitter name (in parentheses)
- Entire tweet (in double quotation marks)
- Date and time of posting
- Medium of publication

> **Example**
>
> `Works Cited`
>
> Smith, Jane (js24notts). "Hoping to visit
>   Paris." 22 Jan. 2015, 9:06 a.m. Tweet.

I18   Emails

Citation order:

- Author (surname, forename)
- Title of message (in double quotation marks)
- Message to (forename surname)
- Date
- Medium of publication

Walters, Fiona. "Re: Event Planning."
Message to Diana Shaw. 24 Sept.
2015. Email.

I19 Visual arts

When citing a sculpture, painting,
photograph or other illustration start with the
name of the artist or creator of the work and
also include the medium and location.

Citation order:

- Artist (surname, forename)
- Title of work (in italics)
- Year
- Medium
- Location

Examples

Works Cited

Gormley, Anthony. *Angel of the North*.
1998. Sculpture. Low Fell, Gateshead.

Martin, John. *The Bard*. 1817. Oil on
canvas. Laing Art Gallery, Newcastle
upon Tyne.

Rodin, Auguste. *The Kiss*. 1882. Marble.
Musée Rodin, Paris, France.

I20 Photographs from the internet

Citation order:

- Photographer (surname, forename)
- Photograph title (in italics)
- Year created
- Photograph
- Website title (in italics)
- Web
- Date accessed

Example

Works Cited

Coils, Malcolm. *Kepier Hospital*. 2014.
Photograph. *Geograph*. Web. 17 Feb.
2015.

I21 Manuscripts or typescripts

If a work has not been published, cite it as a
manuscript (MS) if handwritten, or as a
typescript (TS) if typed.

Citation order:

- Author (surname, forename)
- Title of manuscript (in italics)
- Date
- Medium (TS or MS)
- Collection reference
- Location

Examples

Works Cited

Bunting, Basil. *Materials Towards an
Unpublished Anthology of Poetry*. n.d.
TS. Basil Bunting Archive GB-0033-
BUN/15. Palace Green Library, Durham.

Newton, William. *Letter to William Ord*. 23
June 1785. MS. Ord 324 E11/4.
Northumberland Archives, Woodhorn.

I22 Musical scores

Citation order:

- Composer (surname, forename)
- Title of score (in italics)
- Date of composition
- Place of publication: publisher
- Year
- Medium of publication

Example

Works Cited

Mozart, Wolfgang A. *Don Giovanni: Overture to the Opera*, K 527. 1787. New York: Dover, 1964. Print.

I23 Sound recordings

Citation order:

- Artist (surname, forename)
- Title of recording (in italics)
- Distributor
- Year
- Medium

Example

Works Cited

Brahms, Johannes. *Piano Quintet in F Minor, op.34*. BBC Music, 2015. CD.

I24 Film or video recordings

Citation order:

- Title (in italics)
- Dir.
- Name of director (forename, surname)
- Perf.
- Major performers (forename, surname)
- Distributor
- Year of publication
- Medium of publication

Example

Works Cited

Alien. Dir. Ridley Scott. Perf. Sigourney Weaver, Tom Skerritt, John Hurt. MGM/UA Home Video, 1979. Videocassette.

I25 YouTube videos

Citation order:

- Author's name or poster's username
- Title of image or video (in double quotation marks)
- Name of website (in italics)
- Date posted
- Medium
- Date retrieved

Example

Works Cited

Leponline "Ask the Experts – Plastering a Wall." YouTube. 23 Apr. 2008. Web. 22 Aug. 2015.

I26 Television or radio broadcasts

Citation order:

- Title of episode (in double quotation marks)
- Title of programme (in italics)
- Broadcaster
- Broadcast date
- Medium

Example

Works Cited

"The Day of the Doctor." *Doctor Who*. BBC. 23 Nov. 2013. Television.

I27 Interviews

Citation order:

- Surname, first name of interviewee
- Interview by first name, surname
- Publication title (in italics)
- Date
- Page numbers (if applicable)
- Medium
- Date if accessed online

Examples

Works Cited

Riley, Bridget. Interview by Jonathan Jones. *The Guardian*. 5 Aug. 2015. 33-4. Print.

Corbyn, Jeremy. Interview by Krishnan Guru-Murthy. *Channel 4 News*. 13 July 2015. Web. 12 Sept. 2015.

I28 Personal interviews

If you want to cite an interview you have conducted but not published, use the following:

Citation order:
- Surname, first name of interviewee
- Personal interview
- Date of interview

Example

Works Cited

Palanza, Luis. Personal interview. 26 Nov. 2015.

Sample text

Worsley (*Classical Architecture*) highlighted the variety of styles that eighteenth-century architects employed in their buildings. Initially British architects relied upon the designs of Andrea Palladio, a sixteenth-century Italian architect. His *I Quattro Libri Dell'Archittetura* [*The Four Books of Architecture*] included his re-creations of Roman buildings. As the century progressed, more authentic Roman examples were studied, particularly after the discovery of Pompeii (Nappo). Rich patrons wanted designs in the latest fashion and among those to profit from this demand was Robert Adam, who published his studies of Roman architecture (Adam). With this first-hand knowledge he designed many country houses and public buildings. His work was not always as revolutionary as he claimed (Worsley "Adam as a Palladian"10), but it certainly impressed clients. Peter Leach noted that Adam was even able to take over projects begun by other architects, as at Kedleston in Derbyshire (159). Although most patrons favoured classical styles, Horace Walpole suggested that the Gothic style was 'our architecture', the national style of England (Walpole, cited in Lang 251). Alexandrina Buchanan suggested that Gothic style signified ancient lineage and the British Constitution (43).

Sample list of Works Cited

All sources are listed alphabetically in the list of Works Cited, giving all details of author, title and publication. The first line of the reference is not indented, but subsequent lines are indented by ½ inch (1.3cm), so that authors' names are easily identifiable. End each reference with a full stop. The list of Works Cited for the sample text above would look like this:

Works Cited

Adam, Robert. *Ruins of the Palace of the Emperor Diocletian at Spalatro in Dalmatia.* London: Printed for the author, 1764. *Eighteenth Century Collections Online.* Web. 21 Dec. 2015.

Buchanan, Alexandrina. "Interpretations of Medieval Architecture." *Gothic Architecture and Its Meanings 1550–1830.* Ed. Michael Hall. Reading: Spire, 2002, 27–52. Print.

Lang, S. "The Principles of the Gothic Revival in England." *Journal of the Society of Architectural Historians* 25.4 (1966): 240–67, *JSTOR.* Web. 21 Dec. 2015.

Leach, Peter. "James Paine's Design for the South Front of Kedleston Hall: Dating and

Sources." *Architectural History* 40 (1997): 159–70. Print.

Nappo, Salvatore. *Pompeii: Its Discovery and Preservation.* 2012. Web. 21 Dec. 2015. <http://www.bbc.co.uk/history/ancient/romans/pompeii_rediscovery_01.shtml>.

Palladio, Andrea. I Quattro Libri Dell'Archittetura [*The Four Books of Architecture*]. Venice, D. De Franceschi, 1570. Print.

Worsley, Giles. "Adam as a Palladian." *Adam in Context: Papers Given at the Georgian Group Symposium 1992*. Ed. Giles Worsley. London: Georgian Group, 1993. 6–13. Print.

---. *Classical Architecture in Britain: The Heroic Age*. New Haven: Yale UP, 1995. Print.

NB For more information on using the MLA referencing style, see Modern Language Association (2009) *MLA Handbook for Writers of Research Papers*. 7th edn. New York, NY: Modern Language Association of America.

Section J
Oxford University Standard for the Citation of Legal Authorities (OSCOLA)

Many UK law schools and legal publications use the 4th edition of the Oxford University Standard for the Citation of Legal Authorities (OSCOLA).

Conventions when using the OSCOLA referencing style

- OSCOLA uses numeric **references** in the text linked to full **citations** in **footnotes**
- Very little punctuation is used
- Well-established abbreviations are used for legal sources such as law reports and parliamentary publications. For details of the accepted abbreviations for legal publications, see the Cardiff University *Cardiff Index to Legal Abbreviations* at http://www.legalabbrevs.cardiff.ac.uk/
- OSCOLA assumes that you are referencing UK legal sources. If you are writing about legal material in several countries, use abbreviations of the nations to denote different jurisdictions, for example Deregulation Act 2015 (UK); Homeland Security Act 2001 (USA).

Pinpointing

If you wish to cite a specific page within a source, include this page number at the end of the reference. For example, if you wished to pinpoint something on page 1357 of a report running from pages 1354 to 1372, you would write:

R v Dunlop [2006] EWCA Crim 1354, 1357.

Repeated references and cross-referencing

If you are referencing in your text a source that you have already cited in the footnotes you do not need to give the full reference again. If you are referring again to the previous source, you can use **ibid** (note that this is not italicised). If you are referencing a source earlier than the previous one, use the footnote number of the original reference and a short title or author surname. If you are referencing a different page than the earlier footnote, give the new page number at the end of the new footnote.

Examples
1. *R v Edwards (John)* (1991) 93 Cr App R 48.
2. Ibid 50.
3. CMV Clarkson, *Criminal Law: Text and Materials* (7th edn, Sweet & Maxwell 2010).
4. *R v Edwards* (n1) 53.

NB Footnote 2 uses ibid as it follows immediately after the same source, but directs the reader to a different page. Footnote 4 refers the reader back to footnote 1 (n1) where the full reference is given, but directs attention to what is written on page 53.

How to reference common sources

J1 Books

Citation order:
- Author,
- Book title (in italics and capitalise first letter of each word in title, except for linking words such as and, or, the, for)
- Edition, publisher year (in round brackets)

Example in footnotes

1. CMV Clarkson, *Criminal Law: Text and Materials* (7th edn, Sweet & Maxwell 2010).

J2 Chapters in edited books

Citation order:

- Author,
- Chapter title (in single quotation marks)
- in editor (ed),
- Book title (in italics)
- Edition, publisher year (in round brackets)

Example in footnotes

1. Paul Matthews, 'The Legal and Moral Limits of Common Law Tracing' in Peter Birks (ed), *Laundering and Tracing* (Clarendon Press 1995).

J3 Journal articles

Citation order:

- Author,
- Article title (in single quotation marks)
- Year (use square brackets if it identifies the volume; use round brackets if there is a separate volume number)
- Volume number
- Abbreviated journal title
- First page number

Example in footnotes: with volume number

1. AJ Roberts, 'Evidence: Bad Character – Pre-Criminal Justice Act 2003 Law' (2008) 4 Crim LR 303.

Example in footnotes: with no volume number

2. Po-Jen Yap, 'Defending Dialogue' [2012] PL 527.

J4 Ejournal articles

Citation order:

- Author,
- Article title (in single quotation marks)
- [Year] or (Year)
- Volume number
- Abbreviated journal title
- First page number
- <URL> or <doi>
- accessed date

Example in footnotes

1. Cormac Behan and Ian O'Donnell, 'Prisoners, Politics and the Polls: Enfranchisement and the Burden of Responsibility' (2008) 48(3) Brit J Criminol, 31 <doi:10.1093/bjc/azn004> accessed 14 September 2015.

J5 Bills (House of Commons and House of Lords)

Citation order:

- Short title
- House in which it originated
- Parliamentary session (in round brackets)
- Bill number (in square brackets for Commons Bills, no brackets for Lords Bills)

Examples in footnotes

1. Transport HC Bill (1999–2000) [8].
2. Transport HL Bill (2007–08) 1.

J6 UK statutes (Acts of Parliament)

A change in the citation of UK legal sources took place in 1963. Before this, an Act was cited according to the regnal year (that is, the number of years since the monarch's accession). You may see references to legislation in this format in early publications.

> **Example**
>
> 1. Act of Supremacy 1534 (26 Hen 8 c1).

OSCOLA recommends that when citing all legislation (including earlier Acts) you should use the short title of the Act, with the year in which it was enacted, as shown in the example below.

J6.1 Whole Acts of Parliament

Use the short title of an Act, with the year in which it was enacted.

Citation order:
- Short title of Act
- Year enacted

> **Example in footnotes**
>
> 1. Deregulation Act 2015.

J6.2 Parts of Acts

Citation order:
- Short title of Act
- Year enacted
- s for section number
- Subsection number (in round brackets)
- Paragraph number (in round brackets)

> **Example in footnotes**
>
> 1. Finance Act 2015, s 2(1)(a).

J7 Statutory Instruments (SIs)

Citation order:
- Name/title
- SI year/number

> **Example in footnotes**
>
> 1. Detention Centre Rules 2001, SI 2001/238.

J8 Command Papers

Citation order:
- Author,
- Title (in italics)
- Paper number and year (in round brackets)

> **Example in footnotes**
>
> 1. Lord Chancellor's Department, *Government Policy on Archives* (Cm 4516, 1999).

J9 Law reports (cases)

Which case to cite?

In the UK there is no single publication covering all cases heard in courts. Instead there are many general reports (such as All England Law Reports) and specialist reports (such as Industrial Relations Law Reports) that publish selections of cases. The same case may be reported in several publications, or not reported at all.

If the case is reported in several publications, there is an order of preference for which one to cite in your work. If possible use a citation from one of the Law Reports (Supreme Court/House of Lords, Privy Council Appeal Cases, Chancery Division, Family Division, Queen's Bench) but if these are not available, use the citations (in order of preference) from Weekly Law Reports or All England Law Reports. If a case is not reported in any of these, use the citation for the specialist report or newspaper. The titles of publications are abbreviated in OSCOLA. For details of the accepted abbreviations see the Cardiff University's *Cardiff index to legal abbreviations* at http://www.legalabbrevs.cardiff.ac.uk.

If a case is not reported, give the party names, followed by the name of the court and the date in round brackets.

Citation order:

- Name of parties involved in case (in italics)
- Year (use square brackets if the year identifies the volume, use round brackets if each annual volume is numbered and the year is not required to identify the volume)
- Volume number and abbreviation for name of report and first page of report

> **Example in footnotes: with [Year]**
>
> 1. *Hazell v Hammersmith and Fulham London Borough Council* [1992] 2 AC 1.

NB Date in square brackets because the year identifies the volume required. In this instance, the 2 means that this case appeared in the second volume for the year 1992.

> **Example in footnotes: with [Year]**
>
> 1. *R v Edwards (John)* (1991) 93 Cr App R 48.

NB Date in round brackets because there is also a volume number: this is the 93rd volume of Criminal Appeal Reports.

Neutral citations

From 2002 cases have been given a neutral citation that identifies the case without referring to the printed law report series in which the case was published. This helps to identify the case online, for example through the freely available transcripts of the British and Irish Legal Information Institute (www.bailii.org).

Citation order:

- Name of parties involved in case (in italics)
- [Year]
- Court
- Number of case in that year

> **Example in footnotes**
>
> 1. *Humphreys v Revenue and Customs* [2012] UKSC 18.

This shows that Humphreys v Revenue and Customs was the 18th case heard by the UK Supreme Court in 2012.

If your source uses paragraph numbers rather than page numbers (for example neutral citations) give the citation followed by the number of the paragraph in square brackets:

Humphreys v Revenue and Customs [2012] UKSC 18 [8]

If citing several separate paragraphs, put each in square brackets separated by a comma:

Humphreys v Revenue and Customs [2012] UKSC 18 [8], [14]

If citing several adjacent paragraphs put the first and last numbers in square brackets separated by a dash:

Humphreys v Revenue and Customs [2012] UKSC 18, [15]–[21]

The use of neutral citations does not help with locating cases in printed law reports. You will need to add the citation for the law report after the neutral citation.

> **Example in footnotes**
>
> 1. *Humphreys v Revenue and Customs* [2012] UKSC 18, [2012] 1 WLR 1545.

This shows that the case was reported in the first volume of the Weekly Law Reports for 2012, starting on page 1545.

Citing names of judges

If you wish to quote something said by a judge, include their name in the text associated with the source you are citing:

In *R v Jones*,[7] Williams LJ noted …

If the judge is a peer, you would write, for example, 'Lord Blackstone'. If the judge is a Mr, Mrs or Ms, you would write 'Blackstone J' (J for judge); if a Lord Justice or Lady Justice, you would write 'Blackstone LJ'.

Example in footnotes

7. *R v Jones* [2009] EWCA Crim 120.

J10   *Hansard*

Hansard is the official record of debates and speeches given in Parliament.

Citation order:
- Abbreviation of House
- Deb (for debates)
- Date of debate
- Volume number
- Column number

Examples in footnotes

1. HC Deb 19 June 2008, vol 477, col 1183

- If you are citing a Commons Written Answer, use the suffix W after the column number, for example

2. HC Deb 19 June 2008, vol 477, col 1106W

- If you are citing a Lords Written Answer, use the prefix WA before the column number, for example

3. HL Deb 19 June 2008, vol 702, col WA200

- Use the suffix WS if you are citing a Written Statement, for example

4. HC Deb 18 September 2006, vol 449, col 134WS

- Use the suffix WH if you are citing a debate in Westminster Hall, for example

---

5. HC Deb 21 May 2008, vol 476, col 101WH

- If quoting very old *Hansards*, it is usual, although optional, to include the series number:

6. HC Deb (5th series) 13 January 1907 vol 878, cols 69–70

- In 2007, the earlier system of Standing Committees was replaced by Public Bill Committees. Standing Committee *Hansard* should be cited as:

7. SC Deb (A) 13 May 1998, col 345

The new Public Bill Committees would be cited:

8. Health Bill Deb 30 January 2007, cols 12–15

unless the Bill title is so long that this becomes ridiculous. In this case use:

9. PBC Deb (Bill 99) 30 January 2007, cols 12–15

or, where the context makes the Bill obvious:

10. PBC Deb 30 January 2007, cols 12–15

Since 12 September 2014, written questions and answers have been published in the *Written questions and answers* database (http://www.parliament.uk/business/publications/written-questions-answers-statements/written-questions-answers/) instead of *Hansard*. This means that the column reference is no longer used. Questions and answers in the database are given a number to include in their citation. At the time of writing (October 2015) there was no guidance from OSCOLA for citing written questions and answers. Adapting the format for pre-September 2014 written questions and answers, we suggest:

> **Example of written question and answer (Commons) in footnotes:**
>
> 1. HC 9 October 2015, PQ 9236

> **Example of written question and answer (Lords) in footnotes:**
>
> 1. HL 7 September 2015, HL 1950

In addition, written ministerial statements (which continue to be published in *Hansard*) are also published in the database.

> **Example of Commons written statement in footnotes:**
>
> 1. HC 25 June 2015, HCWS 55

For more information on the use of *Hansard*, see *Factsheet G17: The Official Report* (2010) produced by the House of Commons Information Office. Available at: http://www.parliament.uk/documents/commons-information-office/g17.pdf (Accessed: 14 September 2015).

J11 Legislation from the Devolved Legislatures in the UK

J11.1 Acts of the Scottish Parliament

For Acts of the post-devolution Scottish Parliament, replace the Chapter number with 'asp' (meaning Act of the Scottish Parliament).

Citation order:

- Title of Act including year
- asp number (in round brackets)

> **Example in footnotes**
>
> 1. Scottish Elections (Reduction of Voting Age) Act 2015 (asp 7).

J11.2 Scottish Statutory Instruments (SSIs)

Citation order:

- Title including year,
- SSI number

> **Example in footnotes**
>
> 1. Tuberculosis (Scotland) Order 2005, SSI 2005/434.

J11.3 Acts of the Northern Ireland Assembly

Citation order:

- Title of Act (Northern Ireland)
- Year

> **Example in footnotes**
>
> 1. Ground Rents Act (Northern Ireland) 2001.

J11.4 Statutory Rules of Northern Ireland

The Northern Ireland Assembly may pass Statutory Instruments. These are called Statutory Rules of Northern Ireland.

Citation order:

- Title of Rule (Northern Ireland)
- Year
- SR year/number

> **Example in footnotes**
>
> 1. Smoke Flavourings Regulations (Northern Ireland) 2005, SR 2005/76.

J11.5 National Assembly for Wales legislation

The National Assembly for Wales may pass Assembly Measures (nawm), which are primary legislation but are subordinate to UK statutes.

Citation order:
- Title of Assembly Measure
- Year
- nawm number (in round brackets)

> **Example in footnotes**
>
> 1. NHS Redress (Wales) Measure 2008 (nawm 1).

The National Assembly for Wales may also pass Statutory Instruments. As well as the SI number and year, Welsh Statutory Instruments have a W. number.

Citation order:
- Title of Order (Wales)
- Year
- Year/SI number (W. number)

> **Example in footnotes**
>
> 1. The Bluetongue (Wales) Order 2003 Welsh Statutory Instrument 2003/326 (W. 47).

J12 Law Commission reports and consultation papers

Citation order:
- Law Commission
- Title of report or consultation paper (in italics)
- Number of report or consultation paper, and year (in round brackets)

> **Example in footnotes**
>
> 1. Law Commission, *Double Jeopardy and Prosecution Appeals* (Law Com No 267, 2001).

J13 European Union (EU) legal sources

EU legislation may be legislation, directives, decisions and regulations. The most authoritative source is the *Official Journal of the European Union*.

J13.1 EU legislation

Citation order:
- Legislation title
- Year (in square brackets)
- Official Journal (OJ) series
- Issue/first page

> **Example in footnotes**
>
> 1. Consolidated Version of the Treaty on European Union [2008] OJ C 115/13.

J13.2 EU directives, decisions and regulations

Citation order:
- Legislation type
- Number and title
- Year (in square brackets)
- Official Journal (OJ) L series
- Issue/first page

> **Examples in footnotes**
>
> **Directives:**
> 1. Council Directive 2008/52/EC on certain aspects of mediation in civil and commercial matters [2008] OJ L 136/3.
>
> **Regulations:**
> 2. Council Regulation (EU) 2015/760 on European long-term investment funds [2015] OJ L123/98.
>
> **Commission Decisions** are cited as cases:
> 3. *DS Smith/Duropack* (Case No COMP/M.7558) Commission Decision [2015] OJ C 207/3.

J13.3 Judgements of the European Court of Justice (ECJ) and General Court (GC)

Citation order:

- Prefix ('Case C-' for the ECJ or 'Case T-' for the GC)
- Case registration number
- Case name (in italics)
- Report citation

If you need to pinpoint within the ECR report, use para(s) after the case number.

> **Examples in footnotes**
>
> 1. Case C-111/03 *Commission of the European Communities v Kingdom of Sweden* [2005] ECR I-08789.
>
> 2. Case T-8/89 *DSM NV v Commission of the European Communities* [1991] ECR II-01833, para 132.

J14 International law sources

Guidance on citing international legal sources is given in OSCOLA (2006) *Citing International Law Sources Section*, available at https://www.law.ox.ac.uk/sites/files/oxlaw/oscola_2006_citing_international_law.pdf (Accessed: 25 November 2015).

J14.1 United Nations documents

Citation order:

- Author
- Title
- Date (in round brackets)
- Document number

> **Example in footnotes**
>
> 1. UNSC Res 1970 (26 February 2011) UN Doc S/RES/1970.

J14.2 International treaties

Citation order:

- Title of treaty
- Date adopted (in round brackets)
- Publication citation
- Short title (in round brackets)
- Article number

If possible, cite from the United Nations Treaty Series (UNTS).

When you mention a treaty for the first time in your text give the formal and the short title in brackets. In subsequent references use the short title.

> **Example**
>
> **In-text**
>
> Britain supported the Convention Relating to the Status of Refugees (Refugee Convention)[1] …
>
> **Footnote**
>
> 1. Convention Relating to the Status of Refugees (adopted 28 July 1951, entered into force 22 April 1954) 189 UNTS 137 (Refugee Convention) art 33.

J14.3 International Court of Justice (ICJ) cases

Citation order:

- Case name (in italics)
- Year (in square brackets)
- ICJ report citation or website and date accessed

J15 US legal material

For information on citing and referencing US legal material, see *The Bluebook: a uniform system of citation* (2015) 20th edn. Cambridge, Mass.: Harvard Law Review Association. A useful online guide is Martin, P.W. (2015) *Introduction to basic legal citation*. Available at: http://www.law.cornell.edu/citation/ (Accessed: 14 September 2015).

J16 Personal communications

J16.1 Unpublished emails and letters

Citation order:

- Form of communication
- Author
- Recipient
- Date (in round brackets)

J16.2 Interviews

Citation order:

- Name, position and institution (if relevant) of the interviewee
- Location of the interview and date (in round brackets)

Sample text

The Judge noted the case of *R v Edwards*.[1] The Detention Centre Rules 2001 strengthened this interpretation.[2] An alternative view was suggested by Clarkson.[3] Clarkson highlighted contradictions in the interpretation.[4] Behan and O'Donnell agreed with the Judge's view.[5] They disagreed with Clarkson's opinion on detention.[6] The case left many questions to be resolved.[7]

Sample footnotes

1. *R v Edwards (John)* (1991) 93 Cr App R 48.
2. Detention Centre Rules 2001, SI 2001/238.
3. C M V Clarkson, *Criminal law: text and materials* (7th edn, Sweet & Maxwell 2010) 47.
4. Ibid 56.
5. Cormac Behan and Ian O'Donnell, 'Prisoners, politics and the polls: enfranchisement and the burden of responsibility' (2008) 48(3) Brit J Criminol 31, 37 <doi:10.1093/bjc/azn004> accessed 14 September 2015.
6. Clarkson (n 3) 50.
7. *R v Edwards* (n 1) 49.

Bibliographies

OSCOLA (2012, 4th edn) suggests that for longer assignments such as theses and for books, a separate **bibliography** listing **secondary sources** (everything except legislation and cases) should be provided. Some law schools require that students provide a separate bibliography with all assignments, so check with your tutor if a bibliography is required as well as footnotes.

Authors' names should have surname, then initials of given names (not full given names). This should be in alphabetical order by authors' name. Any works without an author should start with a dash, followed by the title. These unattributed sources are listed at the beginning of the bibliography in alphabetical order by the first major word of the title. A sample bibliography for the examples of secondary sources in this section is:

Behan C and O'Donnell I, 'Prisoners, Politics and the Polls: Enfranchisement and the Burden of Responsibility' (2008) 48(3) Brit J Criminol, 31 <doi:10.1093/bjc/azn004> accessed 14 September 2015.

Clarkson CMV, *Criminal Law: Text and Materials* (7th edn, Sweet & Maxwell 2010).

Law Commission, *Double Jeopardy and Prosecution Appeals* (Law Com No 267, 2001).

Lord Chancellor's Department, *Government Policy on Archives* (Cm 4516, 1999).

Matthews P, 'The Legal and Moral Limits of Common Law Tracing' in Birks P (ed), *Laundering and Tracing* (Clarendon Press 1995).

Roberts AJ, 'Evidence: Bad Character – Pre-Criminal Justice Act 2003 Law' (2008) 4 Crim LR, 303.

NB For more information on using OSCOLA, see Meredith, S. and Nolan, D. (2012) *Oxford University Standard for Citation of Legal Authorities*. 4th edn. and the OSCOLA (2006) *Citing International Law Sources Section*. Available at: http://www.law.ox.ac.uk/publications/oscola.php (Accessed: 14 September 2015).

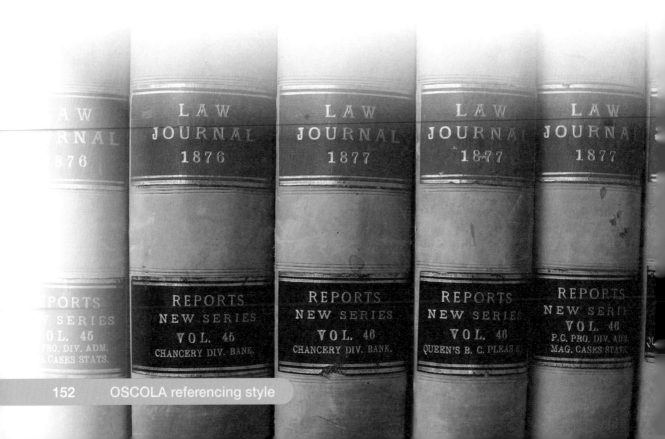

Section K
Vancouver referencing style

The Vancouver referencing style is a numeric citation system used in biomedical, health and some science publications. It was first defined in 1978 at the conference of the International Committee of Medical Journal Editors (ICMJE) in Vancouver, Canada, hence its name. It is now published in Patrias, K. (2007) *Citing Medicine*.

Conventions when using the Vancouver referencing style

- Vancouver uses numeric references in the text, either numbers in brackets (1) or **superscript**[1]
- The same citation number is used whenever a source is cited in your text
- These in-text numbers are matched to full, numbered **references** for each publication in a **reference list**
- The reference list gives publications in the order they appeared in the text, not alphabetically
- Very little punctuation is used
- Well-established abbreviations are used for journal titles.

Multiple citations

- If you have written a section of text based upon several references, these are indicated by listing each source separated by a comma.

> **Example**
>
> Several drug trials (3, 6, 9, 12) proved …

Author names

- Authors should be cited by surname, then initials

> **Example**
>
> Collinton MS.

Note that there is no comma between the surname and initials, nor any period (full stop) after the initials or spaces between the initials. Indicate the end of the author's name with a full stop.

- Authors should be listed in the order shown in the article or book, not alphabetically
- Romanise all author names
- Remove accents and diacritics from letters in author names. For example ñ should be written as n, and Ø written as O.

Multiple authors

- Many science publications are the result of collaborative work, resulting in multiple authors who require citation. If you have six authors or fewer, list all of them, separating their names with a comma. Use a full stop to indicate the end of the authors' names. If there are more than six authors, *Citing Medicine* suggests citing the first six authors followed by et al. or 'and others'.

> **Example**
>
> Bourne AD, Davis P, Fuller E, Hanson AJ, Price KN, Vaughan JT, et al.

Organisations as authors

- Names of organisations are spelt out, not abbreviated.

No authors identified

- If no authors or editors are listed, use the title of the book, journal article or website.

Editors

- Unlike other citation styles shown in *Cite them right*, the Vancouver system never abbreviates the word 'editor'.

Example

Redclift N, Gibbon S, editors. Genetics: critical concepts in social and cultural theory. London: Routledge; 2007.

Edition

- The abbreviation ed. is used for edition.

Example

Bradley JR, Johnson DR, Pober BR. Medical genetics. 4th ed. Malden, Mass.: Blackwell Science; 2006.

Dates

- Dates are given as 'Year' for books or 'Year month (abbreviated) day'.

Article titles

- Article titles follow immediately after the author names
- The article titles are in standard text and are not enclosed in quotation marks, nor italicised or underlined
- Capitalise the first word of the article title, **proper nouns** and initials
- For non-English titles write the title as in the journal article but give a translation in square brackets immediately after the original form

- Use a full stop to indicate the end of the article title.

Journal titles

- Journal titles are abbreviated. If the correct abbreviation is not included in the journal article you have used, check the *National Library of Medicine List of Serials Indexed for Online Users* (http://www.nlm.nih.gov/tsd/serials/lsiou.html). Use a capital letter for each word of the abbreviated title, for example Annu Rev Cell Biol is the accepted abbreviation for Annual Review of Cell Biology.

Book titles

- Only the first word and any proper nouns or acronyms are capitalised and the title is neither underlined nor italicised
- Book titles should be written in their original language. Non-English titles should be followed by a translation of the title in square brackets.

Example

Cite them right: the essential referencing guide.

Reference list and bibliography

- The reference list should only include sources you have cited in your text. List any sources you read but did not cite in your work in a separate **bibliography**.

How to reference common sources in your reference list

K1   Books

Citation order:

- Author/editor
- Title (capitalise only the first letter of the first word and any proper nouns)

- Edition (only include the edition number if it is not the first edition)
- Place of publication: publisher; year of publication
- Pagination (this is optional)

Example: single author

Reference list

Bleakley A. Patient-centred medicine in transition: the heart of the matter. Switzerland: Springer; 2014. 267 p.

Example: up to six authors

Reference list

Nussbaum R, McInnes R, Willard H. Thompson & Thompson genetics in medicine. 8th ed. Amsterdam: Elsevier; 2015.

Example: more than six authors

Reference list

Bourne AD, Davis P, Hanson AJ, Price KN, Vaughan JT, Williams V et al. Health systems. London: Fuller Ltd; 2008. 212 p.

K2   Ebooks

Citation order:
- Author/editor
- Title of ebook (capitalise only first letter of first word and any proper nouns)
- Edition (only include the edition number if it is not the first edition)
- [Internet]
- Place of publication: publisher; year of original publication
- cited year month day (in square brackets)
- Available from: URL

Example

Reference list

Templeton AR. Population genetics and microevolutionary theory [Internet]. Hoboken, (NJ): John Wiley and Sons; 2006 [cited 2015 Dec 23]. 262 p. Available from: http://library.dur.ac.uk/record=b2111435~S1.

K3   Chapters/sections of edited books

Citation order:
- Author(s) of the chapter/section
- Title of chapter/section
- In
- Name of editor(s) of book
- editor(s)
- Title of book
- Place of publication: publisher; year of publication
- Page numbers (preceded by p.)

Example

Reference list

Hart I. The spread of tumours. In: Knowles MA, Selby PJ, editors. Introduction to the cellular and molecular biology of cancer. Oxford: Oxford University Press; 2005. p. 278–88.

K4   Journal articles

Citation order:
- Author(s)
- Title of article
- Title of journal
- Date of publication as year month day;
- Volume (issue): page numbers (not preceded by p.)

Example

Reference list

Consonni D, De Matteis S, Lubin JH, Wacholder S, Tucker M, Pesatori AC, et al. Lung cancer and occupation in a population-based case-control study. Am J Epidemiol. 2010 Feb 1;171(3):323–33.

K5   Ejournal articles

Citation order:

- Author(s)
- Title of article
- Title of journal (capitalise all initial letters)
- [Internet]
- Date of publication as year month day
- [cited year month day];
- Volume (issue): page numbers (not preceded by p.)
- Available from: URL or doi

Example: with URL

Reference list

Amr S, Wolpert B, Loffredo CA, Zheng YL, Shields PG, Jones R. Occupation, gender, race and lung cancer. J Occup Environ Med [Internet]. 2008 Oct [cited 2016 Feb 23]; 50(10):1167–75. Available from: http://journals.lww.com/joem/Abstract/2008/10000/Occupation,_Gender,_Race,_and_Lung_Cancer.12.aspx.

Example: with doi

Reference list

Amr S, Wolpert B, Loffredo CA, Zheng YL, Shields PG, Jones R. Occupation, gender, race and lung cancer. J Occup Environ Med [Internet]. 2008 Oct [cited 2016 Feb 23]; 50(10):1167–75. Available from: doi: 10.1097/JOM.0b013e31817d3639.

K6   Electronic articles published ahead of print

Some scientific publishers are making articles available online before they are available in print, after initial review and corrections but before a final version has been submitted by the author. There may be differences between the published ahead-of-print article and the final published version, so you must distinguish in your reference that you are referring to the earlier rather than the final version.

Example

Reference list

Jarvis-Selinger S, Pratt DD, Regehr G. Competency is not enough: integrating identity formation into the medical education discourse. Acad Med [cited 2016 Feb 23]. ePub ahead of print 2015 Jul 25. Available from: doi: 10.1097/ACM.0b013e3182604968.

Note the use of the qualifying phrase 'ePub ahead of print 2015 Jul 25' in this example, rather than [Internet], in the examples of final published versions above.

K7   Newspaper articles

Citation order:

- Author
- Article title
- Newspaper title
- Edition, if applicable (in round brackets)
- Date
- Section (if applicable)
- Page and column

K8 Newspaper articles on the Internet

- Author
- Article title
- Newspaper title and edition (if applicable)
- [Internet]
- Date
- Date cited (in square brackets)
- Section (if applicable)
- Page and column or approximate location
- Available from: URL

K9 Theses or dissertations

Citation order:

- Author
- Title
- Publication type (in square brackets)
- Place of publication: publisher; year
- Pagination

K10 Conference papers

Citation order:

- Author(s)
- Title of conference paper
- Title of conference (capitalise all initial letters, except for linking words)
- Date as year month day(s)
- Location
- If published, add details of place and publisher or journal reference

K11 Scientific or technical reports

Citation order:

- Author(s)
- Title of report
- Place of publication: publisher; year of publication
- pagination
- Report series and number

K12 Research data collections

Citation order:

- Title of data series
- Title of data collection or programme (capitalise all initial letters, except for linking words)
- Organisation hosting data
- [cited year month day]
- Available from: URL

K13 Organisation or personal internet sites

Citation order:

- Author
- Title of internet site
- [Internet]
- Year that the site was published/last updated
- [cited year month day];
- Number of screens or pages
- Available from: URL

NB For **web pages** where no author can be identified, you should use the title of the web page.

K14 Emails

Citation order:

- Author
- Title of message
- [Medium]
- Message to: recipient
- Date of message [cited date]
- Extent (in square brackets)

K15 Standards

Citation order:

- Publishing organisation/institution
- Standard number
- Title
- Place of publication
- Publisher
- Year

Example

Reference list

British Standards Institution. BS EN 12155:2000. Curtain walling. Watertightness. Laboratory test under static pressure. London: BSI; 2000.

K16 Patents

Citation order

- Inventor
- Assignee
- Title
- Patent country and document type
- Country code and patent number
- Date issued

Example

Reference list

Padley S, inventor. Thompson Hydraulics Ltd, assignee. Pressure isolating valve. United Kingdom patent GB 2463069. 2015 Nov 21.

K17 Photographs

Citation order:

- Artist
- Title
- Medium (in square brackets)
- Place of publication: publisher; date
- Physical description

Example

Reference list

Ikhanov T. Sclerosis in human liver [Photograph]. Kiev: Ukrainian Institute of Medicine; 2015. 1 photograph: colour, 10 x 20cm.

Sample text

More than 38,000 people are diagnosed with lung cancer every year in the UK. (1) Studies elsewhere have investigated links between occupation or socio-demographic status and cancer (2,3), but smoking is the biggest single cause of lung cancer in the UK. (1) Some researchers have analysed populations to establish incidences of tumours. (4) Tumours may spread from the lungs to elsewhere in the body. (5) Charities and self-help groups provide advice and moral support to victims. (1,6)

Sample reference list

1. Macmillan Cancer Support. Lung cancer. [Internet]. 2010 [cited 2015 Aug 23]; [29 screens]. Available from: http://www.macmillan.org.uk/Cancerinformation/Cancertypes/Lung/Lungcancer.aspx

2. Valberg PA, Watson AY. Lack of concordance between reported lung-cancer risk levels and occupation-specific diesel-exhaust exposure. 3rd Colloquium on Particulate Air Pollution and Human Health; 1999 Jun 6–8; Durham, (NC).

3. Amr S, Wolpert B, Loffredo CA, Zheng YL, Shields PG, Jones R. Occupation, gender, race and lung cancer. J Occup Environ Med [Internet]. 2008 Oct [cited 2015 Aug 23]; 50(10):1167–75. Available from: doi: 10.1097/JOM.0b013e31817 d3639

4. Tumour incidences, Nebraska 1973–83. Surveillance Epidemiology and End Results (SEER) Data 1973–2006. National Cancer Institute (USA). [cited 2015 Aug 23]. Available from: http://seer.cancer.gov/resources/

5. Hart I. The spread of tumours. In Knowles MA, Selby PJ, editors. Introduction to the cellular and molecular biology of cancer.

Oxford: Oxford University Press; 2005. p. 278–88.

6. WhyQuit.com. [Internet] 2012 Aug 13 [cited 2015 Aug 23]; [50+ screens]. Available from: http://whyquit.com/

NB For further information on the Vancouver referencing style, see Patrias, K. (2007) *Citing medicine: the NLM style guide for authors, editors, and publishers*. 2nd ed. [Online version updated 11 August 2015]. Available at: http://www.ncbi.nlm.nih.gov/books/NBK7262 (Accessed: 15 September 2015).

Glossary

Address bar: Also known as location or URL bar, it indicates the current URL, web page address, path to a local file or other item to be located by the browser.

Bibliography: A list of all the sources you consulted for your work arranged in alphabetical order by author's surname or, when there is no author, by title. For web pages where no author or title is apparent, the URL of the web page would be used.

Citation: The in-text reference that gives brief details (for example author, date, page number) of the source you are quoting from or referring to. This citation corresponds with the full details of the work (title, publisher and so on) given in your reference list or bibliography, so that the reader can identify and/or locate the work. End-text citations are more commonly known as references.

Common knowledge: Facts that are generally known.

Digital Object Identifier (DOI, doi): A numbered tag used to identify individual digital (online) sources, such as journal articles and conference papers.

Direct quotation: The actual words used by an author, in exactly the same order as in their original work, and with the original spelling. See Section C for details of how to set out all quotations in your text.

Ellipsis: The omission of words from speech or writing. A set of three dots (…) shows where the original words have been omitted.

End-text citation: An entry in the reference list at the end of your work, which contains the full (bibliographical) details of information for the in-text citation.

et al.: (From the Latin *et alia* meaning 'and others'.) A term most commonly used for works having four or more authors (for example Harvard author-date system). The citation gives the first surname listed in the publication, followed by *et al*.

Footnote/endnote: An explanatory note and/or source citation either at the foot of the page or end of a chapter used in numeric referencing styles, for example MHRA. These are not used in Harvard and other author-date referencing styles.

ibid.: (From the Latin *ibidem* meaning 'in the same place'.) A term used with citations that refer to an immediately preceding cited work. It is not used in the Harvard system, where works appear only once in the alphabetical list of references.

Internet: The global computer network that provides a variety of information and communication facilities, consisting of interconnected networks using standardised communication protocols.

In-text citation: Often known as simply the citation, this gives brief details (for example author, date, page number) of your source of information within your text.

op. cit.: (From the Latin *opere citato* meaning 'in the work already cited'). A term used with citations that refer to a previously cited work. It is not used in the Harvard system, where works appear only once in the alphabetical list of references.

Paraphrase: A restating of someone else's thoughts or ideas in your own words. You must always cite your source when paraphrasing (see Section C for details and an example).

Peer review: A process used in academic publishing to check the accuracy and quality of a work intended for publication. The author's draft of a book or article is sent by an editor to experts in the subject, who (usually anonymously) suggest amendments or corrections. This process is seen as a guarantee of academic quality and is a major distinction between traditional forms of publishing, such as books and journals, and information in web pages, which can be written by anyone, even if they have no expertise in a subject.

Plagiarism: Taking and using another person's thoughts, writings or inventions as your own without acknowledging or citing the source of the ideas and expressions. In the case of copyrighted material, plagiarism is illegal.

Proper noun: The name of an individual person, place or organisation, having an initial capital letter.

Quotation: The words or sentences from another information source used within your text (see also Direct quotation).

Reference: The full publication details of the work cited.

Reference list: A list of references at the end of your assignment that includes the full information for your citations so that the reader can easily identify and retrieve each work (journal articles, books, web pages and so on).

Secondary referencing: Citing/referencing a work that has been mentioned or quoted in the work you are reading (see Section A for more details and an example).

Short citation: This is used in numeric referencing systems, including MHRA and OSCOLA, instead of *op. cit.* When a work is cited for the first time, all bibliographic details are included in the footnotes/endnotes and in the bibliography reference. If a work is cited more than once in the text, the second and subsequent entries in the footnotes/endnotes use an abbreviated, short citation, such as the author and title (as

well as a specific page reference), so that the reader can find the full bibliographic details in the bibliography.

sic: (From the Latin meaning 'so, thus'.) A term used after a quoted or copied word to show that the original word has been written exactly as it appears in the original text, and usually highlights an error or misspelling of the word.

Summarise: Similar to paraphrasing, summarising provides a brief account of someone else's ideas or work, covering only the main points and leaving out the details (see Section C for more details and an example).

Superscript number: A number used in numeric referencing styles (including MHRA and OSCOLA) to identify citations in the text, which is usually smaller than and set above the normal text, that is[1].

URL: The abbreviation for Uniform (or Universal) Resource Locator, the address of documents and other information sources on the internet (for example http://...).

Virtual learning environment (VLE): An online teaching environment that allows interaction between tutors and students, and the storage of course documents and teaching materials (see Section E.6 for more details).

Web page: A hypertext document accessible via the World Wide Web (www), the extensive information system on the internet, which provides facilities for documents to be connected to other documents by hypertext links.

Works Cited: The Modern Language Association's (MLA) equivalent of a reference list that provides full details of the sources cited in your text.

Further reading

Avoiding plagiarism

Cardiff University Information Services (no date) *Is it plagiarism quiz*. Available at: https://ilrb.cf.ac.uk/plagiarism/quiz/ (Accessed: 24 September 2015).

Carroll, J. (2007) *A handbook for deterring plagiarism in higher education*. 2nd edn. Oxford: Oxford Centre for Staff and Learning Development.

Cottrell, S. (2013) *The study skills handbook*. 4th edn. Basingstoke: Palgrave Macmillan.

Williams, K. and Carroll, J. (2009) *Referencing and understanding plagiarism*. Basingstoke: Palgrave Macmillan.

Referencing

American Psychological Association (2009) *Publication manual of the American Psychological Association*. 6th edn. Washington, DC: American Psychological Association.

The Bluebook: a uniform system of citation (2015) 20th edn. Cambridge, Mass.: Harvard Law Review Association.

The Chicago manual of style. (2010) 16th edn. Chicago, Ill.: University of Chicago Press.

House of Commons Information Office (2010) *Factsheet G17: The Official Report*. Available at: http://www.parliament.uk/documents/commons-information-office/g17.pdf (Accessed: 27 September 2015).

International Committee of Medical Journal Editors (ICMJE) (2015) *Recommendations for the conduct, reporting, editing and publication of scholarly work in medical journals*. Available at: http://www.icmje.org (Accessed: 27 September 2015).

Meredith, S. and Nolan, D. (2012) *Oxford University Standard for Citation of Legal Authorities*. 4th edn. Available at: http://www.law.ox.ac.uk/published/OSCOLA_4th_edn_Hart_2012.pdf (Accessed: 27 September 2015).

Modern Humanities Research Association (2013) *MHRA style guide: a handbook for authors, editors, and writers of theses*. 3rd edn. Available at: http://www.mhra.org.uk/Publications/Books/StyleGuide/index.html (Accessed: 27 September 2015).

Modern Language Association (2009) *MLA handbook for writers of research papers*. 7th edn. New York, NY: Modern Language Association of America.

Patrias, K. (2007) *Citing medicine: the NLM style guide for authors, editors, and publishers*. 2nd edn. [Online version updated 11 August 2015]. Available at: http://www.nlm.nih.gov/citingmedicine (Accessed: 27 September 2015).

Williams, K. and Carroll, J. (2009) *Referencing and understanding plagiarism*. Basingstoke: Palgrave Macmillan.

Index for the Harvard referencing style

NB To avoid confusion when referencing, this index does not list items specific to the alternative referencing styles (Sections F–K).

Index entries are arranged alphabetically letter by letter, with numbers referring to pages.

Bold numbers indicate glossary entries.

Notes

Notes

Notes